The
Myth of
the Modern
Hero

The
Myth of
the Modern
Hero   Changing Perceptions
of Heroism

JANE L. BOWNAS

sussex
ACADEMIC
PRESS
Brighton • Portland • Toronto

2 4 6 8 10 9 7 5 3 1

First published in 2018 in Great Britain by
SUSSEX ACADEMIC PRESS
PO Box 139
Eastbourne BN24 9BP

Distributed in North America by
SUSSEX ACADEMIC PRESS
ISBS Publisher Services
920 NE 58th Ave #300, Portland, OR 97213, USA

British Library Cataloguing in Publication Data
A CIP catalogue record for this book is available from the British Library.

Library of Congress Cataloging-in-Publication Data
Applied for.

Paperback ISBN 978-1-84519-902-9

Typeset & designed by Sussex Academic Press, Brighton & Eastbourne.
Printed by TJ International, Padstow, Cornwall.

Contents

Preface

This is not a book about heroes. It is rather a book about the ubiquitous use of the word hero and the need people have to transform a minority of their fellow humans into the heroes of myth and legend. This may partly be due to the continuous exposure to heroic tales received by all of us from childhood or to a deep-seated psychological need to convince ourselves that there are people who are capable of performing acts of extreme bravery or altruism and that these people are in some way different from our own inadequate selves. Modern myths have been created by individuals and nations to satisfy this need for role models who perform acts we believe we would be incapable of carrying out.

Perceptions of the hero as warrior and fighter have changed considerably since Homer's depiction of the warrior Achilles in *The Iliad*. In the wars of the twentieth century warrior heroes were not required and a new hero myth was created, that of the patriotic, dutiful and obedient soldier, fighting as part of a group rather than seeking individual glory. However, in post-9/11 America there was a re-emergence of the warrior hero, building on the myth of the superhero who would save America from all external forces which might threaten its position in the world. Heroic myths have been created by new nations eager to lay claim to a heroic past, a mythical past of heroic activism being preferable to a real past of tragedy and defeat. There is often a reluctance to admit that resistance, such as that shown by the Jewish people in Nazi Germany, can be as 'heroic' as armed action.

It is important to recognize that the hero is not necessarily a morally worthy person. In 1930s Germany many people sought inspiration from the old Germanic myths and the belief that a hero would arise who would inspire the German people to fight for a strong, united country, which was culturally and racially pure. The hero they chose was no mythical invention, but someone with fantasies of grandeur, intent on achieving personal power no matter what the cost to Germany and its people.

The word 'hero' is most commonly associated with a person who voluntarily risks their own life for the sake of others. There are many reasons why someone performs a courageous or altruistic act and research studies have been undertaken on the evolutionary origins, biological basis and psychological aspects of extreme altruistic behavior. These studies do not aim to destroy the validity of such acts, but question the belief that the people who perform them are in some way special or superior, rather than being human beings with a particular combination of physical and mental characteristics which enable them to act in this way. Perhaps the most controversial of these studies are those carried out by psychoanalysts who consider that pure altruistic motivation does not exist and that altruistic behavior is merely one of many 'ego defense mechanisms'.

Many problems have been encountered in attempting to award heroic status to an individual, including the necessity for the 'heroic' act to be witnessed, the importance of the psychological make-up and personality of the prospective 'hero', and the problems of 'heroization' and 'retrospective bias'. Some individuals are lauded and honored as heroes whereas others equally worthy and courageous are largely unremembered and unacknowledged.

Each chapter in this book examines a particular category of heroic myth and the whole can be seen as a collection of "stories", mostly real, but a few fictional, all of which serve to question whether the word 'hero' with its origin in myths of the past has now become redundant, and should be replaced by a range of signifiers which more accurately describe the motives and actions of those described as 'heroes'.

Introductory Chapter

The idea of the hero has been embedded in the minds of human beings from the earliest times and across most cultures, but any attempt to attach a particular meaning to the word must meet with failure, for it has been and still is used to represent many different concepts arising out of the societies and cultures in which the idea of the hero is seen to be necessary.

The Greek word *heros* signified a protector or defender of the people and the word was usually used in Greek mythology to signify a warrior. In *The Iliad* Agamemnon addresses the men of the Greek army as *heros*, which is translated by Lattimore as 'fighting men'.[1] Ancient myths reinforced this image of the warrior hero, an image which no doubt inspired many young men to emulate the deeds of Homeric heroes like Achilles. It is significant, however, that Achilles is not considered to be heroic by Plato, who in *The Republic*, advises against using Achilles as a role model in the education of young men, due to his displays of anger, arrogance and his desire for glory and reward.

The depiction of the warrior hero in so many ancient myths leads to a consideration of the meaning of the word myth. For the Greeks the word *mythos* denoted speech or discourse and was associated with the telling of stories. These stories were sometimes based on factual events but were usually imaginative creations which enabled people to make sense of the mysterious and inexplicable phenomena which they experienced both in their own lives and in the world around them. Along with the evolution of extended consciousness and self-awareness in humans came the ability to ask questions and look for meanings, not only about their own existence but about the origin of the earth, the stars and the natural world. From the earliest human societies to the present day, storytellers, poets and artists have used their imaginations in an attempt to provide answers to these questions, and it is hardly surprising that similar themes occur in stories from different cultures and different periods of time for all these stories or myths are attempting to answer the same questions. In George Eliot's novel *Middlemarch*, Casaubon has devoted his life to the impossible task of producing a 'Key to All Mythologies', and many writers and thinkers have similarly attempted to find a common thread running through all myths, aiming to produce a theory which according to Eliot would be 'the doubtful illustration of principles still more doubtful'.[2] The hero myth has featured prominently amongst these would be Casaubons who aim to show that the hero always follows a similar path, meeting similar adversaries and performing similar acts of bravery. These mythical stories of heroes provided role models, giving those living in perplexing and dangerous conditions a sense of significance and purpose in their lives, but these stories were initially handed down by word of mouth and only later in writing, and stories from different times and different cultures do not have as much in common as some mythologists would suggest.

Myths serve to overcome lack of meaning in life, promising a better life after death, positing supernatural beings who are involved in human lives and inventing fantastical stories to explain the creation of the universe. These stories helped to maintain stable and productive societies, based on certain customs, rites and religions, and it was obviously advantageous for the leaders of these societies to encourage belief in these myths. Increasing scientific knowledge in the past few hundred years has provided explanations for many of the phenomena which mystified people in the past, but despite this there are still those who prefer to believe in myths, suggesting that non-rational thought is deep-rooted in the human psyche, or as John Gray aptly puts it 'a life without myths is itself the stuff of myth'.[3]

In 1957, the literary critic and philosopher Roland Barthes published a collection of essays under the title *Mythologies* in which he examined various myths of mass culture, and ended the collection with an essay entitled 'Myths Today'. He begins this essay with the words 'myth is a type of speech' and continues to affirm that because myth is a 'system of communication' it must originate from within history and 'cannot possibly evolve from the "nature" of things'. In other words there may be 'very ancient myths, but there are no eternal ones'.[4] For Barthes a myth is a false belief introduced by those in authority to justify an existing social system and produce a compliant population. He builds on Saussure's system of 'signs' and sees myth as a second order semiological system. For Saussure, linguist and semiotician, the signifier which may be a word or a symbol is associated with a concept which is the signified, and together these constitute a sign. In the formation of a myth this sign becomes in turn the signifier for a new concept and therefore a new sign. Writing in the nineteen fifties when France was still a colonial power, Barthes illustrates this process of myth making using a magazine picture of a black soldier in French uniform, saluting the French flag. The picture is Saussure's signifier, the soldier the signified and together they form a sign. This sign has no other meaning until viewed by an observer who sees this sign as a signifier 'that France is a great Empire, that all her sons, without any color discrimination, faithfully serve under her flag, and that there is no better answer to the detractors of an alleged colonialism than the zeal shown by this Negro in serving his so-called oppressors'.[5] In this way a story or myth is created which is accepted in the same way as ancient myths were and still are accepted, and the myth has transformed a purely historical concept, that is the black soldier saluting the French flag, into a natural concept of French imperialism. In the present century Barthes' description of myth making can be demonstrated in many iconic images resulting from Western and more particularly American intervention in conflicts such as the Iraq war. One particular signifier was the picture of American soldiers placing a United States flag on the statue of Saddam Hussein after the invasion in 2003, possibly without fully realizing the significance of the flag as a symbol of occupation. The resulting sign became a secondary, mythological signifier indicating that it was the power of the United States army and the superior heroism of American soldiers that had brought about the

downfall of Saddam's regime. The possible harmful consequences resulting from the establishment of this myth were
soon realized and the flag was removed, but as Barthes points
out 'myth essentially aims at causing an immediate impression
– it does not matter if one is later allowed to see through the
myth, its action is assumed to be stronger than the rational
explanations which may later belie it'.[6] The Muslim populations of the Middle East had already read the myth as a factual
system rather than a 'semiological system'.

It would appear that in Saussure's first order semiological
system the signifier 'hero' cannot be applied to any one
concept constituting a single sign, but the mythical signifier
'hero' can be applied to many different concepts resulting in
the production of many different signs. The term 'hero' is
therefore a historical concept with no natural meaning
although, as with most myths, the myth of the hero has become
naturalized. Many mythologists would not agree with
Barthes' insistence that myths originate from within history
rather than emerging from the natural world. One of these was
the American writer Joseph Campbell, who achieved considerable fame in the United States after his book *The Hero with a
Thousand Faces* was rediscovered by the film industry in the
1970s, and whose description of the mythical hero's journey
formed the pattern on which many Hollywood films were
based. In his book, which was originally published in 1949, he
affirms 'myth is the secret opening through which the inex-
haustible energies of the cosmos pour into human cultural
manifestation'.[7] He maintains that if all myths originating
from widely different times and places tell the same basic story
and contain the same character types then they must have
arisen from a source outside of historical time. He is somewhat
vague about the nature of this source but in 'The Power of
Myth', the collective title for a series of interviews given in
1988, he suggests that myths serve as a link between the
human and the divine, and speaks of 'the interface between
what can be known and what is never to be discovered because
it is a mystery that transcends all human research'.[8] For
Campbell, God is a 'transcendent energy source . . . the
informing energy of all things'. Campbell's belief in a life force

behind all things is a belief shared by many mythologists, most of whom show a certain mistrust of science, or at least the idea that science necessarily replaces the need for myth. The idea that myths arise from some external source manifesting itself in the consciousness of human beings, something that humans reach out to connect with rather than something which has its origin within the individual human brain, has persisted throughout history. Campbell was particularly influenced by the ideas of the psychiatrist and psychoanalyst, Carl Gustav Jung and his theory of archetypes. Jung proposed that similar themes and character types appear in all ancient myths and also appear in the dreams of all people regardless of cultural background. He considered that these archetypes are passed down from our earliest ancestors and make up what he referred to as a collective unconscious. The mythical hero can be regarded as a particularly significant archetype, and according to Jung this hero archetype has become incorporated into the collective unconscious and becomes manifest in dreams, in which, by becoming the hero, individuals can face and overcome difficulties in their own lives, and achieve goals previously regarded as unattainable. The problem with this theory lies in its attempt to amalgamate two separate phenomena. The fact that psychoanalysts can discern similar themes and similar characters in the dreams recounted to them by their patients does not mean that they originate in some unidentified area of the unconscious mind containing myth-ical stories inherited from our remote ancestors. Jung's division of the unconscious into two parts, the personal and the collective, was very different to Freud's theory of the single unconscious mind containing repressed memories, thoughts and hidden drives like sex and aggression. John Gray, a believer in the necessity of myth for dealing with repressed memories, nevertheless sees that 'myths are not eternal arche-types, stored in a cosmic warehouse. In our time, they are fluid, ephemeral and . . . highly individual'.[9] The idea that uncon-scious archetypes can be brought into consciousness and transformed into images relating to each person's own fears and desires is dependent for its validity on the universality of archetypes, the presumption that they are common to all members of a species and are present from birth. Christian Roesler, himself a Jungian psychotherapist, has made a critical study of the universality of archetypes and concludes that 'there is still no firm scientific foundation for the claim that complex symbolic patterns (as for example the myth of the hero) can be transmitted in a way that every human individual has access to them'.[10] Paradoxically a scientific process, namely epigenetic inheritance, has been adopted by some Jungians in an attempt to acquire validity for his theory, but this has mainly been done without a clear understanding of the mechanisms involved. The term epigenetics refers to the process whereby genes, that is sections of DNA in the nuclei of all our cells, can be switched on or off according to their function or position in the body and this occurs as a result of chemical interactions. It is now known that changes to genes can also occur in response to environmental changes, for example climate, stress, food supply, which can result in chemical changes in the cell. The idea that myths and stories heard by our distant ancestors could, unknowingly to them, be stored in their unconscious brains, that these stored myths are universal for all mankind, and perhaps more importantly can be passed on unchanged through generations, is totally fanciful. Experiences and information from the environment are laid down in the individual brain and stored in the form of neural maps, but a chemical intermediary is necessary if any change in the genome is to occur. Roesler emphasizes the fact that biologists are very clear 'that symbolical information cannot be encoded genetically. Even if it were possible, it would take an enormous space on the genome to encode something like the myth of the hero pattern'.[11]

Cultural information and behavior patterns can of course be passed from one individual to another or from parent to offspring by non-genetic means such as imitation, or, as is the case with myths by story-telling. Evolutionary biologists often use the word *meme* to represent 'a unit of cultural transmission' and demonstrate the extent to which memes can become firmly embedded in the brain. When children are exposed to these myths from infancy it is very difficult, although of course not impossible, for them to be erased. However if these archetypes were to be present in the unconscious brain from before birth, shared by all humans and passed down from generation to generation, it would mean that the considerable body of knowledge acquired by neuroscientists and geneticists on the functioning of the brain and the structure and functioning of the human genome would be rendered invalid.

If it is accepted that myths are invented stories, designed to provide explanations for the various situations in which humans find themselves in a world full of mysteries, or as Barthes would suggest, false beliefs manufactured by those who have power to justify certain social institutions, then it would appear that literature may be considered as part of this system of myth. The Canadian literary critic, Herman Northrop Frye, in his *Anatomy of Criticism* written in 1957, suggests that literature is an extension of mythology and works by using certain laws or formulae derived from ancient myths. In other words all literature embodies archetypes, one of the most important being that of the hero. The fictional hero represents the ideals to which the reader aspires for as Frye admits, 'in every age the ruling social or intellectual class tends to project its ideals in some form of romance, where the virtuous heroes and beautiful heroines represent the ideals and the villains the threats to their ascendancy'.[12] The essential elements of the plot outlined by Frye are basically the same as those described by Joseph Campbell eight years earlier. The hero leaves his ordinary world and undergoes a perilous journey during which he is faced with various tests and conflicts. He then engages in a major struggle against a deadly enemy, as a result of which he becomes transformed and returns to his ordinary world as a changed person. Frye notes that 'the enemy may be an ordinary human being, but the nearer the romance is to myth, the more attributes of divinity will cling to the hero and the more the enemy will take on demonic mythical qualities'. A binary opposition is therefore set up in which 'everything is focused on a conflict between the hero and his enemy, and all the reader's values are bound up with the hero'.[13]

The anthropologist and structuralist Claude Lévi-Strauss, like Frye, considered that literature was governed by rules based on a number of universal themes arising from the unconscious minds of humans, themes similar to those found in all myths. In keeping with Jung's idea of the collective unconscious, Lévi-Strauss claimed that 'myths operate in men's minds without their being aware of the fact', but he provides no explanation for how such a mechanism might operate.[14] In his study of isolated communities he aimed to show that human behavior and the structure of societies followed a pattern and obeyed certain rules which were common to all societies. He maintained that myths were similar across different cultures and interpreted the world by using categories based on binary oppositions, such as male/female, human/animal, high/low, hot/cold, culture/nature, or to follow Frye's example, hero/villain. To counteract criticism that resemblances between groups could be based on past contact he studied isolated, non-literate societies which had no written history and yet which he claimed possessed similar structures and behaviors. His methods and conclusions have been much criticized but his ideas on the place of myth in society are important, if only, as with Jung's idea of the collective unconscious, to provide stepping stones on the path towards a more rational interpretation of the origin and interpretation of myth.[15]

Saussure had introduced the idea that signifiers only have meaning in the sense that they are different from other signifiers and both Northrop Frye and Lévi-Strauss built on this idea in developing their theories that myths interpret the world by using categories based on binary oppositions. Jacques Derrida, writing in the 1960s, believed that in this system of binary oppositions one of the two terms necessarily governed the other and he sought to overturn these oppositions, a process which became known as 'deconstruction'. It can be seen that in a patriarchal society the opposition 'man–woman' places woman as the opposite or 'other' of man and in mythical stories the hero is placed in opposition to the evil villain. I suggest that it is preferable to identify this opposition as that of hero and non-hero. The hero is usually male and is strong, active, brave and adventurous. A series of new oppositions can then be applied in which, as Derrida suggests, one term governs the other. The non-hero is consequently seen as weak, passive, cowardly and risk-averse, whereas the hero is seen as someone to whom we should look up and seek to emulate, an ideal which the ruling class would have an interest in perpetuating. Using Barthe's terminology the word hero is part of a second order semiological system and cannot be used as a signifier for a single sign. As a mythical signifier it can be used to signify any concept which the originator of the myth wishes to convey. In the process of deconstruction the supposed non-hero cannot be viewed as the 'other' of the hero but as someone who does not fit the image of the mythical hero which sections of society aim to promote.

In this book I shall be attempting to 'deconstruct' various myths which have come to be associated with the word 'hero' throughout the twentieth century up to the present day, but it is useful to look briefly at ideas of the heroic which dominated thinking in the nineteenth and early twentieth century.

In his *Philosophy of History* Hegel writes of heroes as 'agents of the World-Spirit' who play a part in determining the course of history and as 'heroes of an epoch' they must 'be recognized as its clear-sighted ones; their deeds, their words are the best of that time'.[16] For Thomas Carlyle, writing in 1842, Hegel's World-Historical man becomes the Great Man of history or the Hero, who Carlyle considered to be an individual possessed of the abilities and skills to influence the course of history. This meant that the hero was not necessarily a military commander like Napoleon but could be 'Poet, Prophet, King, Priest or what you will', although he did consider 'The Commander over Men' to be the most important.[17] Herbert Spencer did not support the Great Man theory of history, maintaining that so-called Great Men were formed by the societies into which they were born rather than arising spontaneously and then being individually responsible for changing those societies. This idea on the role of society in determining how a hero should be defined seems to be in keeping with Barthes' theory of myth formation. The hero is not a product of nature but of history. Spencer also considered that the idea of the hero was encour-aged by stories or myths handed down from primitive societies, and acknowledged that there did seem to be a psychological need for heroes as role models. William James, writing in 1880, disagreed with Spencer's view that individual action alone was incapable of bringing about change in society and believed that there were great men who could initiate change. He introduces a biological aspect to heroism in suggesting that an interaction between genetic and environmental influences might produce individuals who are more likely to perform great or heroic deeds.

Although certainly no admirer of Herbert Spencer, Leo Tolstoy, his almost exact contemporary, certainly shared many of his views on the nature of the hero and expressed these clearly in his great novel of the Napoleonic Wars, *War and Peace*. He writes of 'that false form of the European hero, the imaginary ruler of the people, which history has invented', and comments on how historians have always manipulated facts in order to show their favored commanders as the true heroes.[18]

It is clear that in the nineteenth century the word hero was mainly associated with the so-called great men of history, particularly those who had commanded armies and won battles on behalf of their country. Defeat of Napoleon at Waterloo and expansion of the British Empire left Britain in a dominant position in both Europe and the world, and men like Nelson and Wellington were regarded as national heroes who had saved the nation from defeat. Nelson particularly seemed to possess the traditional heroic characteristics displayed by classical heroes like Achilles, being patriotic and courageous but also interested in personal glory, recognition and the award of medals and honors. Linda Colley writes of 'an ostentatious cult of heroism' which 'served an important propaganda function for the British élite'.[19] These military heroes were not just doing their duty but saving their country and expanding its power, and portraits of the period accentuated this image. Colley sees Benjamin West's painting *The Death of General Wolfe*, although painted more than thirty years before the death of Nelson, as the first of a series of portraits depicting military heroes in this way. It is useful to compare this portrait with the magazine picture of the black soldier saluting the French flag, described by Barthes and used by him as an example of myth creation. Wolfe had died a bloody death during the battle which ended the siege of Quebec and brought about the defeat of the French in Canada. As Colley points out none of the details of the painting are accurate but it enables a second order sign to be created in which the dying Wolfe is seen in a classical, heroic pose, surrounded by officers in British military uniform, with a Union Jack flag above him. Perhaps the most significant image is that of an Indian warrior, kneeling and gazing in admiration at the dying Wolfe, particularly as the native Indians had actually fought with the French. A myth of British heroism, military superiority and imperial power is therefore created in which the hero is shown as bravely sacrificing himself for his country's honor. This myth of the sacrificial hero is carried even further in Arthur William Devis's famous portrait, *Death of Nelson*, in which Nelson is seen as a Christ-like figure who has died to save his country.

It is significant that in the nineteenth century it is only commanders in battle and not the ordinary fighting men who are considered as heroes, although many so-called heroic deeds would have been carried out by anonymous soldiers on the battlefield. This situation does certainly not apply to present-day conflicts, in which it is usually ordinary soldiers who are considered to be heroes, simply for the fact that they have taken part in fighting, particularly if they have been wounded in action. The seeds of this change in attitude may be found in the First World War and the terrible slaughter of millions of young men for what many saw as no obvious reason, together with the perception that some of the commanding generals were incompetent and out of touch with modern warfare.

Nineteenth-century heroes then were principally great men of action and Carlyle's Poet, Prophet or Priest would not have been awarded the accolade of hero. Writing in the middle of the twentieth century the American philosopher Sidney Hook distinguished between heroes of historical action and heroes of thought, and considered that the latter, comprising writers, composers, artists and scientists, could not accurately be described as heroes even though many of them were undoubtedly 'great men'. He admits that the use of the word 'hero' is problematic because of 'the rather large and vague sense given to it in common usage'.[20] One further problem is that the hero is usually seen to be a 'morally worthy' person possessing positive qualities such as courage and altruism. Two figures who changed the course of history in the twentieth century, Stalin and Adolf Hitler, might under Carlyle's definition be considered as 'great men', but it is doubtful whether many would consider them as heroes.

Hook considers that in a modern, democratic society it is necessary to 'break down the invidious distinctions reflected in current linguistic usage between the hero and the masses or the average man'. He suggests that this might be achieved by 'reinterpreting the meaning of the word "hero", and by recognizing that "heroes" can be made by fitting social opportunities more skillfully to specific talents'. He even suggests that a hero may be 'any individual who does his/her work well and makes a unique contribution to the public good'.[21] The days of the great heroes of history are certainly over and the modern 'hero' can be anyone we want them to be. Perhaps the characteristics needed to be recognized as a 'hero' are present in all human beings, emerging when the situation demands, even when this involves living an ordinary life with courage and endurance.

ONE

The Hero as Fighter

Warriors, Soldiers and Martyrs

Throughout the twentieth century and up to the present day men and women have taken on the role of warriors, fighting for their countries, often in distant parts of the world of which they usually have little knowledge, and many of them have been referred to by their compatriots as heroes. Applying the word warrior to a member of the modern armed services may appear to be somewhat perverse, but it would be equally perverse to refer to a mythical Greek warrior like Achilles as a soldier. In this chapter I compare the idea of the modern war hero with the portrayal of Achilles in *The Iliad*, and demonstrate the flexible nature of the signifier 'hero' and its importance as a mythical construct.

Achilles was born to be a warrior, having a human father and the goddess Thetis for a mother. He excels at fighting, and although for most of *The Iliad* his rage against Agamemnon causes him to abstain from joining the battles against the Trojans, he eventually embarks on a horrendous killing spree in order to avenge the killing of his lifelong friend, Patroclus. Achilles' actions are the result of anger, described by Lattimore as 'the anger of pride, the necessary accompaniment of the warrior's greatness'.[1] This anger is part of the Greek quality of *thumos*, which can be seen as 'the spirited part of the psyche' expressed as aggression or courage, the desire for revenge and the longing for honor and glory. It is a basic, primitive emotion acting against reason and its presence can be detected not only in humans but in many animals. It is significant that in *The Iliad* comparisons are often made between warriors in battle and powerful animals, Achilles in particular being likened to a lion, as when the god Apollo says of him 'his purposes are fierce, like a lion who when he has given way to his own great strength and his haughty spirit, goes among the flocks of men, to devour them'.[2] The first line of *The Iliad* emphasizes this anger: 'Sing, goddess, the anger of Peleus' son Achilleus and its devastation, which put pains thousandfold upon the Achaians . . . ' (1: 1–2) It is important to understand that the anger shown by Achilles is not an inherent part of his nature directed in general towards an anonymous enemy. During his argument with Agamemnon in Book One, he makes it clear that he has no personal animosity towards the Trojans, saying 'I for my part did not come here for the sake of the Trojan spearmen to fight against them, since to me they have done nothing' (1: 153–4). He has come to do Agamemnon a favor in helping him to regain his honor for the taking of Helen. His anger or *thumos* arises when Agamemnon threatens to take the captive Briseis from him and he actually ponders whether to 'kill the son of Atreus, or else to check the spleen within and keep down his anger' (1: 191–2). He is visited by the goddess Athene who encourages him to employ reason rather than the basic emotion of anger saying, 'keep clear of fighting, though indeed with words you may abuse him . . . ' (1: 210–11). Achilles, still feeling anger, vows 'never now would he go to assemblies where men win glory, never more into battle . . . though he longed always for the clamor and fighting' (1: 490–2). Later, when Achilles receives the three envoys from Agamemnon, sent in an attempt to persuade him to rejoin the battle against the Trojans, he says 'yet still the heart in me swells up in anger, when I remember the disgrace that he wrought upon me before the Argives' (9: 646–7). Reporting to Agamemnon on their return, Odysseus says of Achilles, 'that man will not quench his anger, but still more than ever is filled with rage' (9: 678–9). However, showing considerable insight, the warrior Diomedes comforts Agamemnon by observing that the proud Achilles 'will fight again, whenever the time comes that the heart in his body urges him to, and the god drives him' (9: 702–3). Both Diomedes and Achilles refer to the 'heart' as being the source of action and spirit accompanied by anger, and it is relevant that 'the heart in his body' is actually Lattimore's translation for the Greek word *thumos*.

Achilles' anger then is raised when he is personally affected by the actions of others, when he feels that he has been insulted, when his pride is injured, but most of all when his friend Patroclus is killed by Hector. In Book Sixteen Patroclus comes to inform Achilles of the plight of the Greeks, their best warriors have been injured and Hector is approaching their ships. He sees that Achilles is still too angry to join the battle and offers to take his place, wearing his friend's armor in the hope that the Trojans will retreat in fear. Overcome by his friend's proposal Achilles seems to be on the point of relenting, claiming 'it was not in my heart to be angry for ever' (16: 60–1), but then remembers his vow not to give up his anger until the fighting actually approached his own ships. Willcock comments that this response demonstrates that 'Achilles, whose fatal anger is the subject of the *Iliad*, is essentially a mild man',[3] an aspect of his character which is indeed demonstrated on several occasions and is perhaps a characteristic not expected of a warrior hero. When Achilles is told of the killing of Patroclus by Hector his first reaction is not anger but extreme grief:

> He spoke, and the black cloud of sorrow closed on Achilleus.
> In both hands he caught up the grimy dust, and poured it over
> his head and face, and fouled his handsome countenance, and
> the black ashes were scattered over his immortal tunic.
> And he himself, mightily in his might, in the dust lay at length,
> and took and tore at his hair with his hands, and defiled it.
> (18: 23–27)

Vowing to kill Hector and knowing that his own death will soon follow, Achilles realizes the futility of his anger against Agamemnon saying,

> I wish that strife would vanish away from among gods and
> mortals, and gall, which makes a man grow angry for all his
> great mind, that gall of anger that swarms like smoke inside of

a man's heart and becomes a thing sweeter to him by far than
the dripping of honey. (18: 107–110)

Although Achilles informs the Greek army and Agamemnon
that he is ending his anger and will rejoin the fighting against
the Trojans, it is obvious that he is referring only to the anger
he has felt towards Agamemnon as a result of his wounded
pride, and that he feels a much greater anger in his heart
towards Hektor, the killer of his friend and cause of his great
grief. In Book Twenty Achilles, 'gathering the fury upon him',
begins his great *aristeia* against the Trojans, culminating in the
killing of Hektor in Book Twenty-Two. An *aristeia* denotes the
domination of the battlefield by a single warrior who excels in
killing the enemy, and Achilles here embarks on an uncon-
trolled killing spree, displaying the utmost cruelty as he
dispatches large numbers of the Trojan army, including
Hector's brother Polydoros. He does, however, reveal the
more reasoning side of his nature when he encounters Lykaon,
a Trojan who he had spared on a previous encounter 'before
Patroclus came to the day of his destiny'. 'Now', he says, 'there
is not one who can escape death',

> So, friend, you die also. Why all this clamour about it?
> Patroklus also is dead, who was better by far than you are.
> Do you not see what a man I am, how huge, how splendid and
> born of a great father, and the mother who bore me immortal?
> Yet even I have also my death and my strong destiny . . .
> (21: 100–110)

Achilles bears no personal animosity towards Lykaon, but he
is a Trojan and a brother of Hektor and must therefore take a
share of the blame for the killing of Patroclus. Achilles
addresses the man he is about to kill as 'friend', for he knows
that despite possessing the qualities of a great warrior hero he
soon will also die and the two men share a common fate. Again
we are shown the complex nature of Achilles' character, the
thumos driven anger and desire for revenge but also the
humanity and intelligence which mark many of his actions.
Above all Achilles desires glory in battle and in his final

pursuit of Hector resents anyone who might come to his assistance for fear they 'might win the glory, and himself come second' (22: 207). The slaughter of Hektor and the degradation inflicted upon his dead body by Achilles is the ultimate representation of the untamed power of *thumos* when it is not subject to reason. Achilles returns to perform the funeral rites for Patroclus and bids farewell to the body of his friend saying,

> All that I promised you in time past I am accomplishing, that I would drag Hektor here and give him to the dogs to feed on raw, and before your burning pyre to behead twelve glorious children of the Trojans for my anger over your slaying. (23: 20–24)

This cannot of course be the end of the story and in the concluding book of the *Iliad* the Greek poet demonstrates that the *thumos* can be tempered by humanity and compassion and the recognition that a common bond exists between all human beings. Achilles is visited by Hektor's father, the old King Priam, who begs for the return of his son's body and asks Achilles to think of his own aged father. Achilles is moved to tears and 'the two remembered, as Priam sat huddled at the feet of Achilleus and wept close for manslaughtering Hektor and Achilleus wept now for his own father, now again for Patroklus. The sound of their mourning moved in the house' (24: 509–512). Hektor is returned to his father and awarded full funeral rites on his return to Troy.

Achilles, a hero of Greek myth, became a role model for young men in ancient Greece, but four hundred years after the writing of *The Iliad* Plato in *The Republic* makes it clear that Socrates did not consider Achilles to be a suitable role model for the education of the Auxiliaries and the Guardians, the warrior and ruling classes in his ideal state.[4] The myth of Achilles must therefore be replaced by a new hero myth which will perpetuate the values of the new city state. Following the critique of some aspects of Homer's poetry at the end of Book Two, Plato commences Book Three with the following statement: 'Morally, most existing poetry is unsuitable because in its representations of gods and heroes it describes, and so encourages, various forms of moral weaknesses'.[5]

One of the characteristics of Achilles which is thought to make him particularly unsuitable as a role model is the possession of *thumos* untempered by reason. Sections of *The Iliad* which emphasize this extreme anger and aggression are to be forbidden and regarded as false, or in Plato's words 'we can believe none of this, and we shall regard as untrue also the whole story of the dragging of the body of Hector round the tomb of Patroclus and the slaughter of prisoners at his pyre'.[6] Other undesirable qualities attributed to Achilles are 'grasping meanness about money and excessive arrogance to gods and men', the former attributed to the fact 'that he took Agamemnon's presents and refused to give up Hector's body unless he was paid a ransome'.[7] Angela Hobbs in her study *Plato and the Hero* considers these criticisms to be unjust, saying 'it is clear that what Homer's Achilles is really interested in is not so much the gifts themselves but the honor that they represent'.[8]

Achilles' lack of discipline and lack of respect for Agamemnon and other army commanders are obviously characteristics that Socrates would not want to be present in members of the civic defense force of his ideal state. As Hobbs notes 'the state needs obedient soldiers, not over-mighty warriors', and also a Philosopher-Ruler rather than a Homeric hero.[9] It seems that Socrates is attempting to introduce a new idea of the hero to accommodate the requirements of his ideal state, and because the young Auxiliaries readily identify with heroes like Achilles they must be taught that these ancient myths are not in fact true. Plato provides further evidence for the falsity of the Homeric myths by exposing the way in which the gods are permitted to commit bad acts and tell lies whereas in his view God is 'without deceit or falsehood in action or word, he does not change himself, nor deceive others, awake or dreaming, with visions or signs or words'.[10]

Achilles then is a warrior who lives for fighting and receives the signifier hero from the Greek word *heros* which signifies a warrior. Those fighting in the wars of the twentieth century would rarely be referred to as warriors but in the present century the word warrior has again come into use, applied particularly to those fighting in the wars which followed the tragic events of September 2001 in the United States. The terrorist attack on the World Trade Centre in New York led to the appearance of a new type of warrior, the American, patriotic, warrior hero, who shares many of the characteristics of the mythical Achilles and is shaped in part by the history of the United States.

The myth of the superhero who would save America from all the external forces which might threaten its supreme position in the world, had its origins in the Cold War period which followed the rise in influence of the Eastern Bloc after the end of the Second World War. Senator Joseph McCarthy, in a speech in February 1950, announced that 'this is a time when all the world is split into two vast, increasingly hostile armed camps' and that America was threatened by 'enemies from within'.[11] There was a fear of world domination by communism and the threat of nuclear war. After the attacks of 11 September 2001 the threat no longer came from communism but from a new ideology which was referred to by the Bush administration as an 'Axis of Evil' which had to be defeated. If force was needed to bring about this defeat then this force was 'in the service of right and peace'.[12] Discussing the response to the events of 9/11, Dan Hassler-Forest considers that these events were perceived as 'a singularity', as an example of exceptionalism or 'the idea that the United States is a chosen nation, a country whose history and unique mission in the world defy comparison'.[13] References were made to 'very American heroes', to the 'larger American family' and to 'one nation indivisible'. Hassler-Forest refers to 'the canonization of these new hero figures that were suddenly recognized in firemen, policemen and rescue workers'. He comments on the focus that was placed on 'individual tales of personal tragedy' rather than on the 'larger geopolitical context', and how any historical meaning attached to the events was reduced to 'familiar narratives' such as 'the difference between good and evil, right and wrong, hero and villain, victim and attacker'. The United States was seen as the innocent victim and the survivors were identified as 'transcendent, mythical heroes'.[14]

It is useful to apply Barthes' ideas of myth formation to the processes occurring after 9/11, with a new mythical signifier being applied to the primary signifier 'hero'. The hero can now be the innocent victim of a terrorist attack or a public servant bravely carrying out his duty, the signifier hero acquiring new historical meanings which have become naturalized. The ideological and political influences which have resulted in the adoption of a particular signifying system are hidden and the myth of the heroic, blameless nation, united and indivisible has been established. This nation has the need for a new type of warrior hero who is fighting to avenge the death of individuals who were part of his American family. War for this warrior has become personal and like Achilles, his anger and hatred is directed towards an enemy who has killed a close friend. He knows that he is on the side of the good and the right against evil and wrong, and because this myth is accepted as part of the natural order he has no need to question it. The war in Iraq, which began in 2003 as a long disputed consequence of the 9/11 attacks, provided the perfect opportunity for this new type of patriotic warrior hero to make an appearance. The twentieth-century wars in Korea and Vietnam were fought to counter the perceived threat to America of an expanding communist ideology, but 9/11 was the first large-scale attack on the American homeland and on innocent American citizens. Those fighting in Iraq were fighting a personal war of vengeance against an enemy who was part of the 'Axis of Evil', an enemy not involved in the attacks of 9/11 but perceived as posing a similar threat to the American people as those terrorists who had flown planes into the Twin Towers.

Someone who exemplified the new type of warrior hero was Chris Kyle, the Navy SEAL, who fought as a sniper in Iraq, was lauded by many in America as a great hero and who recorded his experiences in an autobiography in which he admits to having been trained to 'become a warrior'. It soon becomes apparent that Kyle's thinking is dominated by anger and by an extreme hatred of the enemy. In the Prologue to his autobiography he writes,

> savage, despicable evil. That's what we were fighting in Iraq. That's why a lot of people, myself included, called the enemy "savages". There really was no other way to describe what we

encountered there . . . I only wish I had killed more . . . because
I believe the world is a better place without savages out there
taking American lives'.[15]

In common with Achilles, Kyle's upbringing had endowed
him with the characteristics needed to become a warrior. He
repeatedly lists his priorities in life as being 'God, Country,
Family', and stresses the importance of 'family and traditional
values, like patriotism, self-reliance, and watching out for your
family and neighbors'. He loved guns and hunting and got his
'first real rifle' when he was seven or eight years old. He admits
that he was always 'looking for an excuse to fight', and physical aggression was his immediate response to any perceived
slight.[16] Like Achilles he seems to be controlled by the
thumoeidic side of his nature, which combined with *andreia* or
'manliness' leads to aggression but also to courage. Kyle
admits that SEALS are notorious for getting into bar fights and
pondering on the reason for this admits that 'a lot is owed to
pent-up aggression. We're trained to go out and kill people.
And then at the same time, we're also being taught to think of
ourselves as invincible'.[17] One disturbing characteristic shown
by Kyle which is not shared by Achilles, is his tendency to turn
killing into a game, providing him with a 'fun' experience. On
one occasion he succeeds in killing a group of insurgents who
are attempting to cross a river using large beach balls to keep
themselves afloat. He shoots at the beach balls and laughs as
the men helplessly try to grab hold of the remaining balls but
eventually sink and drown. He comments 'It was kind of fun.
Hell – it was a *lot* of fun'.[18] He admits that he has 'fun' trying
to kill as many men as possible and that he certainly 'enjoyed'
what he was doing. Achilles kills when full of anger but never
just for fun.

The anger which drives Achilles to embark on an uncon-
trolled killing spree, 'that gall of anger that swarms like
smoke inside of a man's heart' (18:109), is caused by the
killing of Patroclus, and for Kyle it is the slaughter of his fellow Americans that drives him to kill. The difference is that
even at the height of his anger Achilles is able to display
humanity and intelligence as when he reasons with the dying

Lykaon, calling him his friend and explaining that he too will soon be dead. Kyle cannot see that the people he kills are fellow human beings, always referring to them as 'savages' as if denying them their humanity. He maintains 'everyone I shot was evil . . . they all deserved to die'.[19] He is, however, capable of showing emotion when his friends are injured or killed and when a particularly close friend is shot and presumed dead he sinks to the ground 'head buried, tears flowing'. He is brought back into action when his chief suggests they 'go get some payback', and like Achilles, his grief is converted into action and aggression.[20]

Kyle's main priorities in life, 'God and Country' or religion and patriotism, are closely related. The playing of the National Anthem and the sight of the Stars and Stripes bring tears to his eyes and he feels in his heart the meaning of 'land of the free' and 'home of the brave'. He says of the people he was fighting in Iraq, 'they hated us because we weren't Muslim. They wanted to kill us, even though we'd just booted out their dictator, because we practiced a different religion than they did'.[21] Later he says 'I didn't risk my life to bring democracy to Iraq. I risked my life for my buddies, to protect my friends and fellow countrymen. I went to war for *my* country, not Iraq. My country sent me out there so that bullshit wouldn't make its way back to our shores'.[22] Kyle admits that he had never known much about Islam although he did know about the Crusades and once when he was home on leave he had a Crusader cross tattooed on his arm. He says 'I wanted everyone to know I was a Christian. I had it put in in red, for blood. I hated the damn savages I'd been fighting. I always will'. Kyle obviously identified with the Crusader warriors fighting to restore Christianity to Muslim lands.[23]

The myth of the patriotic warrior hero fighting to protect a righteous country against an evil enemy is played out in many post-9/11 superhero films, most of which use characters based on characters from earlier films and from comic books of the 1970s and 80s. Kyle's platoon called themselves the Punishers, the name coming from a Marvel comic book character of the 1970s, and a film of the same name which came out in 2004 soon after the start of the Iraq War. Kyle describes the Punisher as 'a real bad-ass who rights wrongs, delivering vigilante justice . . . He killed bad guys. He made wrongdoers fear him. That's what we were all about. So we adapted his symbol – a skull – and made it our own'.[24] They spray-painted the stylized white skull on their vehicles, body armor and guns, and even on buildings and walls to mark their presence. The Punisher may be seen as an anti-hero, certainly not the type of hero that might be recommended as a role model for the young. Unlike characters such as Superman, Batman and Spider-Man, he readily employs murder, violence and torture in his campaigns to defeat those he perceives as evil. The more acceptable superheroes tend to use superhuman powers to defeat evil and protect the public, usually abiding by a strict moral code. Interestingly, Hassler-Forest cites a cartoon which appeared after the 9/11 attacks, showing Spider-Man at Ground Zero and terrified people in the crowd saying 'Where were you? How could you let this happen?'[25] Maybe the type of hero people wanted and needed after the attacks of 9/11 was a figure more like the Punisher, in fact someone like Chris Kyle who enjoyed killing, believed that 'violence does solve problems' and that everyone he shot was evil and 'deserved to die'. Hassler-Forest makes the point that super-hero characters like Superman and Batman are not mythological archetypes 'that may be read as contemporary counterparts to classical figures like Prometheus or Odysseus' but are products of the society from which they emerge and are designed to represent the ideology of that society.[26] They are new mythical signifying systems which in Barthes words 'transform meaning into form'. After 9/11 the American people were looking for a new mythological figure, a true American warrior hero who would save them from the evil threatening them from outside and like the Punisher would employ any means to achieve these ends.

In the *Republic* Socrates recognizes the need for *thumos* in the protection of the state but also sees the dangers that can result from untempered anger and aggression. He believes that 'the primary education of the future Guardians should aim to achieve the correct balance between stimulating the *thumos* and civilizing it' and that 'epic and tragic heroes should be portrayed as calmly courageous and resilient'.[27] Although Achilles is considered to be an undesirable role model he does, on several occasions, demonstrate this civilizing influence which tempers his anger and desire for revenge, as when he shares the grief of Priam over the brutal death of his son. Any such civilizing influence seems to be totally lacking in the actions of Chris Kyle, but there is one occasion on which he comes close to acknowledging the humanity of the enemy. He shoots and kills a young boy who appears to be aiming a rifle at a group of Marines. He describes how 'an Iraqi woman came running up, saw him on the ground, and tore off her clothes. She was obviously his mother'. He immediately checks any feelings of guilt by thinking 'If you loved them, you should have kept them away from the war. You should have kept them from joining the insurgency. You let them try and kill us – what did you think would happen to them'.[28] This passage has a surprising Homeric feel to it and indeed brings to mind Achilles' killing of Priam's younger son, Polydoros, who had been forbidden by his father from taking part in the battle but 'in his young thoughtlessness and display of his running he swept among the champions until thus he destroyed his dear life' (20: 411–12).

It is essential that the quality of *thumos* which fills men with the spirit to fight when their family or country is threatened is capable of being suppressed when its expression would be inappropriate. For the warrior whose life is devoted to fighting and killing this may be problematic and requires the conscious decision to employ reason and self-discipline. Kyle, who admits that 'fighting is a fact of life when you're a SEAL', cannot control his inclination to respond aggressively to any perceived insult and when home on leave he becomes involved in many fights resulting in several court appearances. The *thumoedic* side of his nature is obviously not confined to the battlefield. Although adopted by many Americans as the perfect American warrior hero, Kyle would certainly not be regarded by Socrates as a role model to be emulated by the young.

Neither Achilles nor Kyle possess the qualities which Socrates considers to be essential for defenders of his ideal state. To fulfill this role they need to suppress their desire for individual glory and become obedient warriors, learning to control excessive or inappropriate *thumoedic* impulses by subjecting them to reason and discipline. The problem with this for the warrior hero is that his heroic status depends on the achievement of glory in battle even though this may result in his death. Angela Hobbs, commenting on Achilles' blood-lust in battle and yet his awareness of the possibility of death, says 'an acute consciousness of one's mortality will mean that to some extent the *thumos* will *have* to go temporarily mad in order to overcome its aversion and perform the dangerous or self-sacrificial acts by which heroic fame is won'.[29] Socrates disapproval of any display of excessive aggression or self aggrandizement by the warrior hero was derided by Nietzsche who admired Homer's idea of the life force as a force of nature, as when Achilles is compared to a fierce lion with a 'haughty spirit' who 'goes among the flocks of men, to devour them'. Nietzsche introduces a similar analogy, in which he shows the absurdity of calling birds of prey evil for attacking 'good' little lambs, saying 'to require of strength that it should *not* express itself as strength, that it should not be a wish to overpower, a wish to overthrow, a wish to become master . . . is just as absurd as to require of weakness that it should express itself as strength'.[30] Hobbs comments that 'Nietzsche portrays the Homeric hero as one of the most vital manifestations of the will to power' and 'contrasts 'Homeric' values with what he sees as the enfeebled, life-denying, rational values of Plato'.[31]

Chris Kyle, the American patriotic hero, does possess some of the characteristics of the Homeric warrior hero, but is certainly not a member of Nietzsche's 'aristocratic race'. Rather than being motivated by the 'will to power', which Nietzsche sees as life enhancing and ennobling, he is moti-vated by anger, hatred and the desire to kill. Various interpretations have been made of Nietzsche's 'will to power', but in examining the characteristics of the warrior hero 'rampant for spoil and victory', Robert Solomon's comment is particularly apposite:

thinking of Will to Power as self-mastery, including self-discipline, self-criticism, even self-denial, gives a much better handle on Nietzsche's conception than the warrior metaphors that he often employs.[32]

When Nietzsche speaks of war and warriors he is not exhorting people to take up arms on behalf of the state but conversely, to wage war against the laws, ideas and values imposed on the individual from outside. The enemy can be seen as anyone attempting to impose or normalize their own ideas, or can even be one's own self if tempted to accept these ideas. He says,

> I welcome all signs that a more virile, warlike age is about to begin, which will restore honor to courage above all. For this age shall prepare the way for one yet higher, and it shall gather the strength that this higher age will require some day – the age that will carry heroism into the search for knowledge and that will wage wars for the sake of ideas and their consequences.[33]

This higher age will require higher human beings who have won the battle over their own mediocrity, in other words the *Übermensch* or 'overman'. It is perhaps unfortunate that the word *Übermensch* is frequently translated as 'Superman', a word more recently associated with the patriotic super-hero, fighting to protect the values of his society and representing the ideology of that society.

Chris Kyle, like the superheroes of American culture, embodies a myth created by a society to represent the requirements of that society at a particular time in history. At the beginning of the twentieth century there was no need for such a myth. In Britain the defeat of Napoleon and the subsequent dominance of the British navy had removed any threat of invasion, and there was no menacing foreign ideology which might appear to pose a threat to British society. In the years leading up to the First World War, Britain, the United States, and most of the countries of Europe did not have the need for warrior heroes. There were factors which might lead to disputes between nations such as 'economic rivalry', 'the scramble for colonies', and 'the alliance system dividing Europe into unfriendly camps', yet none of these alone would have been sufficient to cause so many countries to engage in such a deadly and lengthy conflict.[34] The quarrel was not between the peoples of the participating countries but between their political and military leaders, who feared loss of influence and power. Many of these leaders were incapable of making correct decisions when required, were afraid to break alliances made many years previously, and particularly in the case of Germany were eager to expand their military influence in Europe. The soldiers who fought in the First World War were not fighting to avenge the deaths of members of their family or country, and unlike warrior heroes were not passionate about fighting and killing. On the outbreak of war a new myth had to be created and it was the image of the patriotic, dutiful and obedient soldier which contributed to a new definition of the hero, defined by his allegiance to his country and its leaders, unquestionably obeying their commands.

In his comments on war and warriors, Nietzsche says, 'I see many soldiers: if only I could see many warriors! What they wear is called uniform: may what they conceal with it not be uniform too!'[35] The wearing of a uniform identifies the soldier as a representative of a particular country and as a member of a group, each member being similarly molded by the state for the purpose of fighting and overcoming an enemy. The soldier cannot act as an individual but must carry out the orders of his commanders and ultimately, the state. Although Nietzsche is using the soldier as an example of uniformity it is clear that his comments also apply to the masses of people who live their lives according to the dictates, aspirations and moral codes of the state,

> Only there, where the state ceases, does the man who is not superfluous begin: does the song of the necessary man, the unique and irreplaceable melody, begin.[36]

At the beginning of the First World War a poster was produced showing Lord Kitchener, the secretary of State for War, in his military uniform, pointing his finger at the potential recruit, over the words 'Britons: Lord Kitchener Wants You. Join Your Country's Army! God Save the King'. As with Barthes' example of myth formation, this image acts as a secondary mythological signifier indicating that anyone who does not respond is cowardly, unpatriotic and disloyal to their country and their King. Patriotism and loyalty were all that mattered and the majority of those who responded had little understanding of who the enemy was and why they were fighting. Relations between Britain and the German Empire had been reasonably good and George V and Kaiser Wilhelm II were both grandsons of Queen Victoria. In his poem 'England to Germany in 1914', Thomas Hardy writes,

> Is it that Teuton genius flowers
> Only to breathe malignity
> Upon its Friend of earlier hours? . . .
> We have nursed no dreams to shed your blood,
> We have matched your might not rancorously . . . [37]

and in 'The Pity of It' he comments on the similarity between the Wessex local dialect and German, condemning those ' . . . who flung this flame between kin folk kin tongued even as are we'.[38] The aggressiveness of Germany's military leaders and British propaganda served to arouse patriotism and a sense of duty in the young men who enlisted but there was no sense that the people they were fighting belonged to an alien culture which threatened the lives of ordinary people.

The disciplined, respectful soldier was expected to be a team member, fighting in a group rather than seeking individual glory, in fact the type of soldier Socrates considered to be desirable in his ideal city-state. The *aristeia* performed by Achilles in which he individually dominates the battlefield demonstrating his prowess and warrior-like qualities would not be required on the battlefields of the First World War. Instead, Lloyd George, in a speech made in September 1914, introduces the concept of the sacrificial hero, saying,

> The stern hand of fate has scourged us to an elevation where we can see the great everlasting things which matter for a nation –

the great peaks we had forgotten, of Honor, Duty, Patriotism, and clad in glittering white, the great pinnacle of Sacrifice pointing like a rugged finger to Heaven.[39]

A new hero myth is created, that of the soldier who endures suffering and sacrifices his life for his country. The soldier has become a victim, the expression of the *thumoeidic* side of his nature only becoming evident under conditions of extreme danger when his life is threatened.

Perhaps one of the greatest portrayals of the soldier as victim is that given by Erich Maria Remarque in his novel *All Quiet on the Western Front*, based on his own experiences on the German front line in the summer of 1917. Unlike the situation in Britain where the army depended on volunteer soldiers for at least the first year of the war, conscription was already present in Germany and many of the young men being sent to the Western Front came straight from the classroom. They had given no thought to joining the army and felt no particular aggression towards or hatred of the enemy they were being sent to fight. They had an ideal and romantic view of war but ten weeks of army training left them 'embittered, and finally indifferent', recognizing that what mattered was 'not intelligence but the system, not freedom but drill'. Individual personality had to give way to group mentality and in the words of the narrator, Paul Bäumer, 'we were to be trained for heroism as though we were circus-ponies'.[40] Heroism is now a group attribute exhibited by obedient, compliant soldiers fighting as a unit rather than individually, in an army made up of submissive soldiers rather than mighty warriors.

Thumos, the primitive, aggressive response to danger, is very much in evidence on the front line:

> At the sound of the first droning of the shells we rush back, in one part of our being, a thousand years. By the animal instinct that is awakened in us we are led and protected. It is not conscious; it is far quicker, much more sure, less fallible, than consciousness. One cannot explain it . . . It is this other, this second sight in us, that has thrown us to the ground and saved

us, without our knowing how. If it were not so, there would not be one man alive from Flanders to the Vosges.

We march up, moody or good-tempered soldiers – we reach the zone where the front begins and become on the instant human animals.[41]

During a particularly fierce engagement the German soldiers come face to face with the French, and Paul finds himself gazing into the eyes of a French soldier he is about to kill and for a moment cannot throw his grenade 'into those strange eyes' that are fastened on him. As with any animal that is threatened, however, self preservation becomes all important and he throws the grenade. He says,

We have become wild beasts. We do not fight, we defend ourselves against annihilation. It is not against men that we fling our bombs, what do we know of men in this moment when Death is hunting us down . . . we feel a mad anger . . . that fills us with ferocity, turns us into thugs, into murderers, into God only knows what devils.[42]

The soldier as thug and murderer or as an automaton, 'power-less, madly savage and raging', does not fit the image of the soldier as mythical hero fighting bravely for his country. It is tempting to see a parallel here with the 'madly savage and raging' warrior Achilles, as he performs his *aristeia*, but Achilles is not powerless and is not fighting in self defense but to avenge the death of his friend. He is filled with *thumos* but can still exert a measure of control over his primitive, animal-istic response, and unlike the soldiers on the Western front he personally knows most of the men he kills. Remarque, like Homer, reveals in vivid detail the horrors of the battlefield. Beside him is a lance-corporal who 'has his head torn off. He runs a few steps more while the blood spouts from his neck like a fountain'. Later a young Frenchman 'puts up his hands, in one he still holds a revolver – does he mean to shoot or to give himself! – a blow from a spade cleaves through his face'.[43] The first Trojan Achilles kills during his *aristeia* meets a similar fate. He 'struck him with the spear as he came in fury, in the middle of the head, and all the head broke into two pieces' (20: 386–7). He stabs another Trojan in the temple and 'the bronze spearhead driven on through smashed the bone apart, and the inward brain was all spattered forth' (20: 398–400). Achilles' spear passes through the body of the young Polydoros, and as he fell he 'caught with his hands at his bowels in front of him' (20: 418). Paul sees similar horrors on the Western Front: 'men living with their skulls blown open', soldiers who 'run with their two feet cut off' and another who 'over his clasped hands bulge his intestines'.[44] Achilles, the warrior, cannot be expected to feel compassion for those he kills, but he is fully aware of his actions and revels in his power and strength. Paul, on the contrary, experiences a sense of complete helplessness, controlled solely by his animal instinct for survival. He says 'we are forlorn like children, and experienced like old men, we are crude and sorrowful and superficial – I believe we are lost'.[45] These soldiers kill because they are following the commands of their superiors, not through hatred or a desire for vengeance. The camp for the German soldiers is next to a Russian prison camp and Paul becomes aware of their common humanity: 'It is strange to see these enemies of ours so close up. They have faces that make one think – honest peasant faces . . . they look just as kindly as our own peasants in Friesland . . . A word of command has made these silent figures our enemies; a word of command might transform them into our friends'.[46] Paul comes very close to viewing his enemy as a friend when he stabs a French soldier who has fallen into a shell-hole where he is sheltering from machine-gunfire. The gurgling noise from the soldier suggests to Paul that he is dying but he takes a long time to die and Paul, crawling towards him, gazes into the eyes of his enemy which are fixed upon him. He feels an urge to help him, to ease his suffering, and gives him muddy water to drink and attempts to bandage his wounds. Eventually the soldier dies and Paul talks to him, saying,

> Comrade, I did not want to kill you . . . but you were only an idea to me before, an abstraction that lived in my mind . . . It was that abstraction I stabbed. But now, for the first time, I see you

are a man like me . . . Forgive me, comrade . . . why do they never tell us that you are poor devils like us.[47]

Paul takes the soldier's pocket-book containing photographs of his family and promises to write to his wife. He says, 'Comrade . . . today you, tomorrow me . . . but I will fight against this, that has struck us both down'.[48] Like Achilles saying to Lycaon as he kills him 'even I have also my death', Paul acknowledges the common fate of himself and the French soldier he kills, but Achilles the warrior willingly and consciously takes the life of his enemy and does not regret his action. For Paul the killing is a primitive, *thumoeidic* response necessary for his own survival, but for Achilles the performing of his *aristeia* is his means of avenging the death of his friend and achieving glory and honor as a warrior. The twenty-first century warrior Chris Kyle not only kills willingly but gains pleasure from the act of killing. The common bond of humanity felt by both Paul and Achilles with the enemy they kill is completely absent in Kyle.

During a pause in the fighting the Kaiser comes to visit the German troops to distribute Iron Crosses and the young soldiers wonder if the war would have happened if the Kaiser and other leaders 'had said No'. They discuss the absurdities of war such as the fact that both sides are fighting to 'protect their fatherland' and that 'professors and parsons and newspapers' on both sides 'say that the right is on their side'. They see that wars start when one country offends another but that it is not the people of these countries who offend each other only the state leaders and rulers, many of whom profit from war.[49] In Britain, Lloyd George, by no means an advocate for war, had said in a speech in 1911 that,

if a situation were to be forced upon us in which peace could only be preserved by the surrender of the great and beneficent position Britain has won by centuries of heroism and achievement . . . then I say emphatically that peace at that price would be a humiliation intolerable for a great country like ours to endure.[50]

At the end of the war Lloyd George hopes to 'make Britain a fit country for heroes to live in', but when the soldiers of the First World War returned home most of them were not greeted as 'heroes'. As Remarque says at the end of *All Quiet on the Western Front*,

> Now if we go back we will be weary, broken, burnt out, rootless, and without hope. We will not be able to find our way any more. And men will not understand us . . . we will be superfluous even to ourselves, we will grow older, a few will adapt themselves, some others will merely submit, and most will be bewildered; – the years will pass by and in the end we shall fall into ruin.[51]

These men were not warriors who lived for killing and they were certainly not heroic figures, if being heroic meant fighting willingly for a cause in which they believed and for which they were willing to die. Homer's description of Achilles during his *aristeia* paints a picture of the vengeful warrior intent on achieving glory,

> . . . before great-hearted Achilleus the single foot horses
> trampled alike dead men and shields, and the axle under
> the chariot was all splashed with blood . . .
> . . . The son of Pelius was straining
> to win glory, his invincible hands spattered with bloody filth.
> (20: 498–503)

When Paul stabs the Frenchman who has fallen into his shell-hole there is no feeling of glory, only shame at the deed he has committed,

> I notice my bloody hand and suddenly feel nauseated. I take some earth and rub the skin with it; now my hand is muddy and the blood cannot be seen any more [52]

Perhaps these two images encapsulate the difference between the warrior and the soldier and also the nature of the mythical signifier 'hero' which, as I have discussed, has been applied to many different concepts and has no natural meaning. Achilles is a mythical hero and is used by Homer to demonstrate the importance of honor and glory in the life of the Greek warrior. The soldiers fighting in the wars of the twentieth century may also be seen as mythical heroes, the signifier 'hero' now referring to the patriotic soldier, unquestioningly loyal to his country and its leaders, but in reality fighting for his own survival in horrendous conditions.

A third type of fighter to whom the signifier 'hero' has been applied is the guerrilla or freedom fighter, usually operating in small groups against a perceived or actual oppressor. Unlike the soldier who usually fights on behalf of the state the guerrilla fights to overthrow the current state apparatus or to liberate his country from an outside oppressor. This will usually involve fighting against a larger regular army. An exemplar of the changing use of the mythical signifier 'hero' over a fairly short period of time arises from a study of the conflict between the Palestinians and Israelis in the years between the end of World War Two and the present day. The Armistice which ended the Arab–Israeli War in 1949 left Israel in control of large areas of the former Palestinian territory and many Palestinian Arabs were forced to flee to neighboring countries, large numbers of these refugees settling in camps in neighboring Lebanon. In 1964 the Palestine Liberation organization was founded to represent the Palestinian people, their goal being the liberation of Palestine through armed struggle. The members of this organization took part in guerrilla warfare and were seen by many Palestinians as warrior heroes. It would be a mistake however to equate these guerrilla fighters with self-styled warriors such as Chris Kyle who fight on behalf of the state against a threatening foreign ideology. The guerrilla fights to protect his homeland from an oppressor and fights in small groups against a much larger traditional army. These groups are usually composed of armed civilians rather than trained soldiers and often contain women as well as men. Referring to the Palestinian freedom fighters in the 1960s and 1970s Laleh Khalili says,

> Taking up arms and joining one of the political factions was considered not only a matter of national pride but also a much-

needed vocation, when even low-paying jobs were nearly unattainable for Palestinians. While prosaically the guerrilla would also be a bread-earner, he (or increasingly she) also became the warrior of the family, a source of familial pride and prestige, perceived as restoring the lost honor of the community through a mythico-heroic presence.[53]

These fighters referred to themselves as *fida'iyyin*, the original Arabic translation of which is warrior or fighter but in more recent times has been defined as 'one who sacrifices himself for his country'. Claire Norton notes that 'the Arabic definition does not necessarily connote suicide troops, but may instead describe brave heroic troops prepared to do their bit and make the ultimate sacrifice, as many allied troops did in the Second World War'.[54] Khalili also points out that the fact that the Palestinian fighters chose to refer to themselves as *fida'iyyin* rather than *mujahideen*, which is translated as 'holy warriors', 'subtly points to a religion-neutral, even secular, notion of self-sacrifice'.[55] The period from 1969 until 1982 was seen by exiled Palestinians, particularly those living in overcrowded camps in Lebanon, as a period of heroic resistance, the heroes being the gun carrying guerrilla fighters. In 1982 Israel invaded Lebanon and as a result of heavy bombing in Beirut the *fida'iyyin* were forced out of the camps and gradually replaced by a group who had a rather different approach to heroic resistance. Khalili describes how

> the departure of guerrilla fighters . . . downgraded the importance of self-preservation as a fundamental element of resistance . . . contributed to the demise of the elite heroic figure of the fighter . . . and the emergence of Hizbullah – whose ideology of resistance relied on martyrdom as both a means to an end and as an end in itself.[56]

The signifier 'hero' was no longer applied primarily to the guerrilla fighter, it was now the self-sacrificing martyr or *shahid* who was awarded heroic status. The Palestinians in exile knew that the regaining of their homeland by armed resistance could never meet with success against the might of the Israeli army, and they now sought heroes who were willing to sacrifice themselves for the sake of the people as a whole. It is perhaps difficult for the Individualist Westerner to understand the eagerness with which martyrdom is performed, but in a Collectivist society the individual life is of little importance compared with the interests of the group, and for a follower of Islam it is an essentially religious act which cannot be performed by a non-believer. The word *shahid* is translated as 'witness', and the martyr becomes a witness for their faith, ensuring for themselves a place in Paradise. The *shahid* does not necessarily choose martyrdom and may be the unintentional victim of violence, unlike the *fida'yi* whose heroic status is always associated with active participation in conflict. Khalili, in her study of the developing emphasis on martyrs after the invasion of Lebanon in 1982, says,

> The *shahid* in everyday Palestinian usage is not only the active dissident dying in the act of resistance, but also the innocent bystander, not necessarily armed and engaged in the act of fighting, who is however killed at the hands of the unjust oppressor . . . the common denominator is death at the hand of the enemy.[57]

There is a correspondence here with the response to the attacks of 9/11 in America, when the innocent victims of the attacks were referred to as 'heroes' because they had died at the hands of the enemy, or while carrying out their duty as firemen or policemen. The people who committed the act of terrorism had chosen martyrdom, but those who died as a result of their actions were also referred to as martyrs by many in the United States, even though they had not willingly sacrificed themselves for a cause or for their faith. The mother of one of the Muslim victims of 9/11 was quoted as saying 'the true martyrs of 9/11 were not the men who piloted planes into buildings, but their victims',[58] and some supporters of the terrorists considered that the many innocent Muslim bystanders who were killed in the attacks should also be thought of as martyrs. The apparent confusion in the use of the words 'hero' and 'martyr' exemplifies the flexible nature of these words and how mythical signifiers are created to conform to the wishes of a particular group or state. Describing the commemoration of heroes and violent events by exiled Palestinians, Khalili says,

> Iconization transforms a concrete event, object or being into a symbol. It is the process by which an event is decontextualized, shorn of its concrete details and transformed into an abstract symbol, often empty, which can then be instrumentalized as a mobilizing tool by being "filled" with necessary ideological rhetoric.[59]

This process of iconization can be seen to parallel Roland Barthes' theory of myth formation in which Khalili's 'concrete event, object or being' transformed into an 'abstract symbol' is equivalent to Saussure's primary sign for a particular concept being transformed into a secondary sign in the process of myth formation. Khalili's 'abstract symbol' can be used as a tool to put forward a particular ideology just as Barthes' secondary sign can be used by a social or political system to promote an ideology. His example of the image of the black soldier saluting the French flag being used to legitimize the idea of empire is a particular example. Khalili suggests that in the commemoration of a violent event such as a battle during the Palestinian struggle, the details such as suffering, loss and often defeat are ignored and the entire event is commemorated as an example of courage and heroism and filled with 'ideological rhetoric'.

Claire Norton's study of 'interpretive naming' during the Iraq War is a further example of myth formation aimed at influencing the perception of the participants on both sides. She says,

> The naming of the enemy in the 2003 Gulf War is not isomorphic with reality, but rather provides an instance of interpretative naming. In other words, the nouns used to signify the enemy represent more than is initially obvious and includes an element of covert interpretation. By labeling and thus characterizing the recipient, texts are framed and narratives constructed. Naming

also conditions the expectations of audiences and guides their subsequent interpretation.[60]

During the war the American and British combatants were described as soldiers, marines, special forces etc., indicating that they were 'representatives of a legitimate state institution; the army . . . licensed to carry out limited acts of aggression in the interests of the state'. In contrast the Iraqi combatants were referred to as paramilitary, militias or terrorists, in other words irregulars not acting on behalf of a legitimate state. The war therefore becomes a war against terrorists rather than against a sovereign nation state. A further development was the use of the word *fedayeen* to describe the Iraqi fighters, an Arabic word which, as I have described, referred initially to a warrior or fighter and not to a martyr or suicide attacker. Norton suggests that the emphasis on definitions which refer to sacrifice and martyrdom indicates that

> these particular definitions have been selected not because this is what the phrase means but rather because it is the interpretation which accords with the dominant narrative of the war. By naming these combatants as martyrs or those ready to sacrifice themselves a link is made to the terrorist tactics of suicide bombers in Israel and Palestine and ultimately to the attacks on the Twin Towers.[61]

The use of the word *fedayeen* therefore establishes a link with terrorism and Islamic fundamentalism and legitimizes the war as 'part of the greater war on terror'.

Norton's emphasis on the importance of naming in the Iraq War is corroborated by Chris Kyle when he discusses the use of conscripted Iraqis to fight alongside the American troops. He refers to these men as *jundis*, the Arabic word for soldiers and labels them as being 'pathetic' and 'incompetent', and certainly not heroes. The use of the word soldiers for these conscripts and others who were previously members of Saddam's army and have deserted or surrendered, implies that 'the legitimate army of Iraq is, if not allied with the American and British, then at least acquiescent with their goal of the liberation of Iraq'.[62] Those who do fight are insurgents, terrorists or paramilitaries and the war therefore becomes legitimized. Kyle spends some time defining the various names used for the 'variety of terrorist forces' fighting in Iraq. He says,

> There were Fedayeen, members of a paramilitary resistance group . . . there were small, poorly organized groups of Iraqi guerrillas, who were also called Fedayeen . . . though nearly all were Muslim, nationalism rather than religion tended to be their primary motive and organizing principle. Then there were the groups organized primarily around religious beliefs. These identified themselves as mujahedeen, which basically means "people on jihad" – or murderers in the name of God . . . There was also al-Qaeda in Iraq, a mostly foreign group that saw the war as an opportunity to kill Americans.[63]

Kyle does indicate a difference between the *fedayeen* and religiously motivated *mujahedeen*, a difference which Norton suggests was deliberately disregarded, but his use of the term does point to a disorganized group of terrorists with no connection to the official government. The Fedayeen Saddam were actually a paramilitary, non-religious organization set up by and loyal to Saddam Hussein and played a large part in resisting the advance of Coalition forces. They disbanded after the fall of Baghdad but many of their members did join smaller guerrilla forces. The *mujahedeen* did not form in Iraq until after the invasion and increased their attacks during the years of occupation. It does not therefore seem reasonable to refer to these 'jihadi murderers', as Kyle does, in an attempt to justify the initial invasion. The 9/11 hijackers were known members of al-Qaeda and so to link this terrorist organization with Saddam Hussein's government would provide justification for the invasion as a war against terrorism. Many reports produced by intelligence agencies in both America and Britain since the invasion have indicated that there was no evidence of a link between Saddam Hussein and al-Qaeda and that this group only appeared in Iraq as a response to the invasion. By linking known terrorist organizations with Iraq a myth was created which, being legitimized by the state for its own purposes, was generally accepted as the true state of affairs. In accordance with Barthes' theory of myth formation, 'the myth consumer takes the signification for a system of facts: myth is read as a factual system, whereas it is but a semiological system'.[64] So ready was the population of the United States in particular to accept this myth, that they regarded the soldiers sent out to fight in Iraq as warrior heroes fighting against the terrorists who had planned to attack their country and people, or in the words of Chris Kyle 'the savages out there taking American lives'.

In this chapter I have attempted to demonstrate how the word 'hero' is used as a mythical signifier which has no natural meaning. In recent times this signifier has been applied almost universally to the service men and women fighting in their countries' armies in distant lands, regardless of their individual performance in action or whether they are injured or killed. These men are not warriors like the mythical Achilles, who lives for fighting and aims to achieve individual glory, although they are frequently referred to as warriors by veteran and family support groups in Britain and America.[65] They are soldiers, paid to fight for their countries, fully aware that they will be placed in dangerous situations which may result in serious injury or death. Their motives may be patriotism, a sense of duty, a desire to avenge the deaths of fellow countrymen or even a desire for adventure and comradeship. As with the soldiers of the First World War they carry out the orders of their commanding officers, fight instinctively for their own survival and for the survival of other members of their team, and ultimately hope to return safely to their homes and families. The application of the word 'hero' to all servicemen and women fighting in foreign wars raises the question of what is actually being signified by the use of this word and whether its use says more about those who use it than those to whom it acts as a signifier. As Umberto Eco writes,

> The real hero is always a hero by mistake; he dreams of being an honest coward like everybody else. If it had been possible he

would have settled the matter otherwise, and without blood-shed. He doesn't boast of his own death or of others'. But he does not repent. He suffers and he keeps his mouth shut; if anything, others then exploit him, making him a myth, while he, the man worthy of esteem, was only a poor creature who reacted with dignity and courage in an event bigger than he was.[66]

Although he uses the word 'hero', Eco seems to be admitting that the word is actually meaningless, or only acquires meaning for those who use it as a mythical signifier. Most people are capable of performing actions which are later considered to be heroic, but only a few are placed in situations which require such actions. We endow the fighting soldier with so-called heroic qualities because he performs actions we feel we would be incapable of, and yet in reality he is only a 'poor creature' like us, reacting with 'dignity and courage'.

Guerrilla fighters like members of the Palestine Liberation Organization were regarded as heroes by the exiled Palestinian people because they were prepared to fight for their homeland, something which the majority of people would be incapable of doing. They took on the role of protectors and defenders who would save their people from the threat of extinction. With the failure of armed resistance, heroic status was transferred to martyrs, who became heroes either by committing acts of suicide or just by being present during violent confrontations which resulted in their deaths. As Laleh Khalili discovered when visiting the Lebanese camps, these martyrs are commemorated by 'powerful and evocative' images in the form of posters, photographs and murals which serve to iconize those who are portrayed. She adds 'the canonization of certain martyrs as archetypal ones, and the emergence of martyrs' mothers as iconic figures in commemorative practices have all been crucial elements in the promotion of martyrs as heroes'.[67]

The use of images of American servicemen and women after 9/11 similarly became widespread in the United States. William Astore notes,

Ever since the events of 9/11, there's been an almost religious veneration of U.S. service members as 'Our American Heroes' . . . in local post offices, as well as on local city streets here in central Pennsylvania, I see many reminders that our troops are "hometown heroes." Official military photos of these young enlistees catch my eye, a few smiling, most looking into the camera with faces of grim resolve tinged with pride at having completed basic training.[68]

These young people are turned into heroes even before they have seen action on the battlefield.

A further aspect of myth formation in relation to heroism has been described in connection with the exiled Palestinian community, but can also be seen in many communities who have suffered oppression, namely passive resistance or 'heroic endurance'. This will be the subject of my next chapter.

TWO

Heroic Resistance

Courage and Steadfastness

The word heroic has been used as a signifier for a wide variety of activities, including fighting for one's country in wars, displaying exceptional courage and bravery, sacrificing one's life to save others and even for performing outstandingly at sporting activities. Those involved in these activities are referred to as heroes primarily because they perform actions that most of us feel we would be incapable of carrying out. There is another type of behavior which is sometimes referred to as heroic but does not depend on physical strength or activity, and this is heroic resistance or to use the Arabic word, *sumud*, meaning steadfastness.

Laleh Khalili observes that the memoirs and literary works of many prominent Palestinian writers 'obscure the hope, the steadfastness, and the sheer resilience of the refugees in the years immediately following the *Nakba*, and instead point to these years as the years of humiliation, stasis and nihilism'.[1] A similar attitude is frequently encountered in relation to the years following the Israeli invasion of Lebanon in 1982, when the 'heroic' fighters of the Palestinian Liberation Organization were forced out of the camps and active resistance was no longer possible. As Khalili makes clear, the people in the camps did not just give up and face obliteration, but adopted a 'strategy of survival' which was 'not submission'. They held onto their homes and land concentrating on day-to-day survival in the camps, maintaining an attitude of hope rather than despair. The way they conducted 'the daily affairs of life – provisioning of food, protecting the peripheries of the camp, even speaking in a Palestinian accent which may mark the speaker out for harassment at checkpoints – all became acts of political resistance against the Lebanese army and militias'.[2] The fact that some Palestinians do not recognize this resistance as heroic is a consequence of the association of this word with active resistance usually carried out by young men with guns. The survival of the Palestinian communities in Lebanon after 1982 depended largely on the efforts of women who were determined to rebuild their homes and maintain their family structures. It is, of course, unnecessary to speak of such behavior as 'heroic', as however oppressive or horrific the situation may be most human beings will react to preserve their own lives and those of the group to which they belong. The *thumos* which comes to the fore at the height of battle when the soldier is fighting to preserve his own life and that of his companions, is the same spirit or energy which becomes manifest when family or community is threatened and is part of man's basic primitive nature evident in most animals. Those Palestinians who emphasize the importance of armed resistance point to the history of their people and a 'national ancestry of revolt and heroism' which is partly mythical but is used 'to counter the equivalent Israeli claim to the land on the basis of quasi-biblical history'.[3] Both Palestinians and Israeli Zionists may be said to invent a heroic past in order to justify their claims to the establishment of a nation-state. Both groups prefer to look back on a mythical past of heroic activism than to accept a tragic past consisting of a long series of trials and tribulations.

One heroic myth in particular was created and developed during the establishment of the state of Israel, namely the myth of Masada.[4] The mountain top fortress of Masada was occupied in AD 66 by a group of Jews determined to resist the occupation of Judaea by the Romans. In AD 72 the Roman army besieged the fortress expecting to meet resistance, but when they entered they found the bodies of nearly one thousand Jews who had committed suicide rather than face capture by the Romans. This incident would have been unrecorded and unremembered if it had not been for a record of the event made by the Jewish historian Josephus Flavius in his book *The Wars of the Jews*. No other account of the siege exists and Josephus' original Aramaic version was lost, all knowledge of the event being obtained from a Greek translation preserved by the early Christian Church. Yael Zerubavel notes that the story of Masada 'did not vanish from the records of Jewish history, but it disappeared from the Jews' collective memory', and it was only with the rise of Zionism at the end of the nineteenth century that 'the ancient Hebrews' wars of national liberation assumed a special symbolic significance'. A new Hebrew translation of Josephus' account of the Masada siege was published and according to Zerubavel this was 'a highly selective representation of the historical record . . . emphasizing certain aspects of Josephus' account and ignoring others'.[5] One aspect of this new translation was the naming of the Masada Jews as Zealots, a prominent group of Pharisees who had fought continuously against Roman rule but from which arose a far more violent and extremist group called the Sicarii. According to the Josephus account it was this group, well known for brutally murdering Jewish collaborators as well as Romans, who occupied the fortress at Masada. The mythical interpretation infers that the besieged Jews fought bravely against the Roman army but there is no mention of this in the original account, which makes it clear that when invasion of the fortress was seen to be inevitable, the leader of the Jewish rebels, Elazar ben Yair, ordered his men to kill their wives and children and then to slaughter each other. The fact that Jewish law forbids suicide, maintaining that it is only God who has control over life and death, would help to explain why the mythical narrative avoids the mention of a mass suicide and prefers to see Masada as a 'historical metaphor for a national struggle for freedom and the readiness to fight for it to the bitter end'. Zerubavel quotes several historians from the pre-state period in Israel who write of the Masada people who 'fell in battle' and fought 'until the very end', and ordinary Israeli Jews who describe Masada as 'a liberation war, a heroic war, a war of few against many . . . ', and of people 'dying holding their weapons'. The myth of Masada in which a military defeat and mass suicide was turned into a story of active heroism and patriotism was important before and immediately after the establishment of the state of Israel, but since the 1970s many

Israelis have become aware that the episode may have been misinterpreted, and that in fact very little is known about what actually happened at Masada.

The Masada myth assumed particular significance during and in the years immediately following the Second World War, when news of the persecution and slaughter of European Jews reached the Jewish community in Palestine. Zerubavel, in her comparative study of the reaction to the Masada myth and to the Holocaust in Europe, writes of 'the glorification of the Masada people as a counter-model for the Holocaust victims' and that 'side by side with expressions of anxiety over the fate of European Jews, there was a tendency to criticize the victims' passive behavior'.[6] There is an interesting parallel here with the views of those Palestinian Arab writers who looked back on the years of exile in Lebanon as 'years of humiliation, stasis and nihilism'. The Jewish people living in what was perceived as exile in Europe were regarded by some as living a 'life of exile, dependence, humiliation, slavery and degradation'. These words were spoken in 1943 by David Ben-Gurion, the first Prime Minister and founder of the State of Israel, who in the same speech contrasted these exiled Jews with the Zionist settlers who would choose to die with weapons in their hands rather than suffer such humiliation.[7] Again, as with the exiled Palestinians, the fact that the European Jews did not on the whole respond to persecution with armed resistance did not mean that they passively accepted their fate. Interestingly no official Holocaust memorial day was introduced in Israel until 1959, and as Zerubavel points out the Israelis 'maintained a dual classification that defined the armed resistance to the Nazis as "heroic" and assigned the "Holocaust" to the "nonheroic" aspects of the Jews' experiences'.[8] Particular emphasis was placed on commemorating the 'heroic' actions of those involved in the Warsaw Ghetto uprising, which some referred to as the 'Masada of Warsaw', and it was only after hearing the personal testimonies of Holocaust survivors during the trial of Adolf Eichmann in 1961 that the Israeli people began to realize that the European Jews had not meekly accepted their fate and gone 'like sheep to the slaughter'.

The association of the word 'heroic' with action, particularly armed action, leads to a very narrow and misleading interpretation of the Holocaust and fails to acknowledge the widespread resistance shown by the European Jews to the threat of mass extinction. In fact, when examining the various forms of resistance employed, it becomes clear that the use of the word 'heroic' is totally inappropriate when describing the actions of those who often knew they were to die under the most horrendous conditions, had no thought of receiving recognition for their actions, but refused to submit willingly to their oppressors. In many cases refraining from action resulted in the survival of many who would otherwise have been killed in reprisal actions. Martin Gilbert, whose history of the Holocaust was published in 1986, spent seven years collecting material for his book from survivors, eye-witnesses, diaries, contemporary records, official documents, testimonies given at the Nazi war crimes trials and many other primary sources.[9] I make no apology for making use of these sources in exploring the nature of both active and passive resistance in a situation which unlike Masada is not based on myth.

Armed resistance, considered to be 'heroic' by the Israeli Jews, was not often possible due to the unavailability of firearms. However, as the German army advanced through Eastern Europe, many Jews armed themselves with knives, sticks, or any other implement that could be used as a weapon. These weapons were often needed to resist attacks from local populations who welcomed the opportunity to attack and eliminate the Jewish communities who had lived amongst them for hundreds of years. Gilbert records an incident at Lubieszow in Ukraine in June 1941 when,

> Jews armed themselves with axes, hammers, iron bars and pitchforks, to await the arrival of local Ukrainians intent upon murder as soon as the Red Army withdrew, and before the Germans had arrived. The Ukrainians came and were beaten off. But then, retreating to the nearby village of Lubiaz, they fell immediately upon the few isolated Jewish families living there. When, the following morning, the Jews of Lubieszow's self-defense group reached Lubiaz, 'they found the bodies of twenty

children, women and men without heads, bellies ripped open, legs and arms hacked off'.[10]

When the Germans arrived in the village they 'hunted down and destroyed the local Jews who had dared to resist their attackers'. Reprisals often involved the killing of large numbers of innocent Jews. In August 1941 a German policeman was shot dead by a member of the local Jewish resistance movement near Pinsk in Ukraine and 'as a reprisal, 4,500 Jews were liquidated' by the Einsatzkommando unit in the area.[11] In another incident,

> an Einsatzkommando unit drove more than two thousand Jews, among them 710 men, 767 women and 599 children, into a ditch. Suddenly, a Jewish butcher jumped up, seized one of the German soldiers, dragged him into the ditch, and sank his teeth into the German's throat with a fatal bite. All two thousand Jews, including the butcher, were then shot.[12]

As the German army advanced across Europe many such incidents were recorded and in consequence it is hardly surprising that the local Jewish communities had to think twice before carrying out acts of resistance. Although, as with soldiers encountering the enemy on the battlefield, the immediate human reaction is to fight back, there is also the need to protect and preserve the lives of one's family and community. A greater degree of courage might be required to resist the natural impulse to take action against the aggressor when such action will result in the deaths of others. Such passivity might not be considered 'heroic' by those who associate the signifier 'hero' with outward bravery and action rather than inner courage and steadfastness.

As was the case with Masada, the need for 'heroes' may sometimes affect the way in which a particular event is remembered and recorded, and occasionally may result in a complete distortion of the truth. One report published in an underground newspaper in March 1942 referred to an event which occurred in the town of Nowogrodek in eastern Poland the previous December, in which five thousand Jews were forced from their homes and executed in a local ravine. The newspaper wrote,

> In the city of Nowogrodek there were two hundred Jews who refused to go to the execution site like beasts driven to the slaughter. They found the courage to rise, weapon in hand, against Hitler's hangmen. Although they all fell in the unequal fight, before their own death they killed twenty of the murderers . . . In wonder and respect we bow our heads at the grave of the heroes of Nowogrodek. They are a symbol of the end to surrender and slavish obsequiousness. They are a symbol of the proud bearing of human beings who wish to die as free men.[13]

Gilbert notes that this act of resistance 'has been shown by historical research to be a myth', and it is important to understand why the writer of this account found it necessary to manufacture this myth and why it was so enthusiastically welcomed by the Jews in Warsaw. The image of the Jewish resistors rising with 'weapon in hand' as opposed to meekly surrendering with 'slavish obsequiousness' echoes completely the image created by the perpetrators of the Masada myth, and shows a complete misunderstanding of the realities of the situation in which the Jews of Nowogrodek were brutally murdered. This need for the demonstration of active resistance is based on a false understanding of so-called heroism, and a belief that the hero figures of ancient myths, together with more recent historical 'heroes', should always be admired and emulated. Emmanuel Ringelblum, the historian of the Warsaw ghetto, replies to those who questioned the apparent lack of resistance in the Jewish communities,

> Of no use will be the lies that are being fabricated about Nowogrodek or the recent ones about Kowel; in no place did Jews resist the slaughter. They went passively to death and they did it, so that the remnants of the people would be left to live, because every Jew knew that lifting a hand against a German would endanger his brothers from a different town or maybe from a different country . . . Not to act, not to lift a hand against Germans, has since then become the quiet, passive heroism of

the common Jew. This was perhaps the mute life instinct of the
masses, which dictated to everybody, as if agreed upon, to
behave thus and not otherwise.[14]

Perhaps, as the report suggests, we should 'bow our heads at
the graves of the heroes of Nowogrodek', not because they
died with weapons in their hands, but because they demonstrated the courage to die with equanimity so that the lives of
others would not be endangered.

Many Jews of course did resist, for in the face of danger or
imminent death the individual instinct to fight and survive
takes over from rational thought. Chaim Kaplan another
Warsaw Jew who recorded events in his diary, writes of two
unarmed Jewish porters who, when facing death by shooting,
attacked and struggled with their German killers, but were
eventually overcome. He writes 'on the morrow, the Nazis
avenged the mutiny of the two porters with 110 Jews. They
were put to death for the sins of men who had never laid eyes
on them'.[15]

July 1942 saw the start of the forced transportation of
European Jews to Treblinka the extermination camp in Eastern
Poland. This process was referred to by the Nazis as 'resettlement' and some have questioned why large numbers of Jews
appear to have passively accepted their fate and boarded the
transport wagons without resistance. Apart from the fact that
any who did resist would be immediately shot, many Jews,
despite rumors to the contrary, actually did believe that they
were to be resettled on land further east or were being taken
to work in factories. It is understandable that they would have
found it impossible to believe the fate that actually awaited
them in the gas chambers of Treblinka and the unimaginable
evil that would be perpetrated by the Nazis upon innocent
men, women and children. Franciszek Zabecki, a Polish
railway worker at Treblinka station, reported on scenes he
witnessed as the wagons arrived,

Moans, shouts, weeping, calls for water or for a doctor issued
from the wagons. And protests: 'How can people be treated so
inhumanly?' 'When will they let us leave the wagons alto-

gether?' Through some air gaps terrified people looking out, asking hopefully: 'How far is it to the agricultural estates where we're going to work?'[16]

In the Warsaw ghetto people were enticed onto the trains with the offer of 'a free issue of three kilogrammes of bread and one of jam for any families that would go voluntarily to 'resettlement'. They were also reassured 'that families would not be separated'. These were desperately hungry people dying from starvation in the ghetto and the prospect of being able to give their children bread could not easily be turned down. As Ringelblum wrote, these were people 'driven by hunger, anguish, a sense of hopelessness of their situation' people who 'had not the strength to struggle any longer'.[17] He writes of talking with a refugee 'who had been hungry for a long time. All his thoughts were occupied with food. Everywhere he went, he dreamed of nothing but bread . . . but at the same time he had grown apathetic, nothing mattered to him any more'. Ringelblum concludes 'perhaps this physical passiveness, a direct result of hunger, is a factor in the silent, unprotesting wasting away of the Jewish populace'.[18] David Wdowinski, one of the resistance leaders in the ghetto, recalls that many of those boarding the transport wagons were asking themselves 'If over there things were not so bad, and here we have to live in hiding and suffer hunger, and since we can be together with our families, why not go?' He adds 'entire families, bag and baggage gave themselves up. And indeed, they were not separated. They were gassed all together'.[19]

Wdowinski, a psychiatrist and neurologist, was a leader of a resistance organization called the Jewish Military Union or ZZW, which operated within the Warsaw ghetto. Despite expressing sympathy with those who innocently boarded the trains to Treblinka, Wdowinski and the members of the ZZW believed in armed resistance and played a large part in the ghetto uprising which occurred the following year. The ZZW was an essentially right-wing group in sympathy with the Revisionist anti-Communist Zionist movement and mainly made up of former officers of the Polish army. It was joined in the ghetto by members of the youth movement Betar which had been formed in Latvia in the 1920s and shared the philosophy of the ZZW. Its members wore military uniforms and had received training for military action. The name Betar refers to the last Jewish fort to fall to the Romans in AD 136, when a Jewish revolt was crushed by the Romans leaving 580,000 Jewish fighters dead and bringing an end to the Jewish–Roman wars. Unlike the case of Masada there are several historical documents which verify the events occurring at Betar, and although it is recognized by the Israelis as an example of armed heroic action it has not been similarly adopted as a site of pilgrimage, probably due to its situation close to disputed West Bank territory.[20]

The other resistance organization active in the Warsaw ghetto was the Jewish Combat Organization or ZOB, set up in July 1942 at the time of the first deportations from the ghetto by young Jews from various pioneer youth movements, who were mainly anti-fascist and pro-Communist. It was this resistance group, which was consequently considered by post-war Israelis to epitomize the concept of heroic action and to be the true heirs of Masada. The need for 'heroes' after a catastrophe as great as the Holocaust is understandable, but in the case of the Warsaw ghetto fighters it was also necessary for them to be the 'right sort of heroes'.

Libionka and Weinbaum in their analysis of the role played by the two resistance organizations note that 'for the first decades after the war, the Israeli political and social ambience was largely determined by those who were ideologically closer to the ZOB than the ZZW. Undoubtedly the ruling Labor movement used its control over national institutions to promote the story of those with whom it sympathized'.[21] Most books, documents and films made after 1945 glorified the heroism of the ZOB fighters and made virtually no mention of the role played by the ZZW. Martin Gilbert mentions the first meeting of the newly formed ZOB in July 1942, at which they questioned how they would be able to resist the Germans when they had no weapons. They decided to link up with other ghettos 'to prepare joint schemes, to smuggle arms and individuals, and to pass on messages and funds'.[22] Gilbert makes no mention of the ZZW although its members were present in the ghetto at the time of the formation of the ZOB, and Libionka and Weinbaum note that the ZZW was 'generally mentioned in passing, mainly as a small group that played only a nominal role in the actual fighting or simply fled the ghetto when it began'.[23] It is significant that Emmanuel Ringelblum, who was actually present in the ghetto at the time of the uprising, writes 'why is there no information on the ZZW in the history. They must leave an imprint, even if in our eyes they are unsympathetic'. He describes a visit to the ZZW headquarters before the outbreak of the uprising and 'was clearly impressed by the group's substantial arsenal and supply of German uniforms' and the significant role they played in the action.[24] Further evidence as to the 'heroic' role played by the ZZW is provided in German documents which indicate that 'the heaviest battle of the uprising was fought on Muranowska Square – precisely the sector of the ghetto in which the ZZW was concentrated'.[25]

In a talk given to the Irish Jewish Historical Society in April 2013, Yanky Fachler, the author, businessman and writer on the Holocaust, recalls evidence given by a Polish woman, Alicja Kaczynska, who had lived on Muranowska Street outside the ghetto and opposite the ZZW headquarters. She recalls that when the Germans entered the ghetto in April 1943, it was the heavily armed ZZW fighters who offered the greatest resistance, confirming the evidence given in the German documents found after the war. She also describes witnessing two flags raised by the ZZW over the ghetto, the blue and white Jewish flag and the red and white Polish flag.[26] Libionka and Weinbaum confirm that 'it is widely acknowledged that Jewish and Polish standards were flown over the ZZW headquarters, arousing the ire of the Germans and the admiration of many of the Polish bystanders'.[27]

Despite this evidence most accounts of the uprising undervalue the role played by the ZZW and maintain that it was members of the ZOB who played the major part in resisting the German army. In Lucy Dawidowicz's widely praised book, *The War against the Jews*, published in the 1970s, she gives a very different account of the raising of the flags in the ghetto: 'ZOB fighters remained exultant, their morale high. On one roof they flew the red and white Polish flag alongside the Jewish blue and white banner'.[28] Dawidowicz claims to have obtained information about the uprising from one of the leaders of the ZOB, Yitzhak Zuckerman, and yet in his own memoirs he says 'anyone who tries to attribute the flags to the ZOB is distorting them and history'.[29] Elsewhere in her book Dawidowicz claims that it was 'only the left-wing parties and the socialist Zionist youth movements' who transformed themselves into 'functioning underground organizations'.[30] Dawidowicz was not alone in presenting this somewhat one-sided view of the Warsaw ghetto uprising, the main reason for this being that for many writers and researchers the only material available to them was the large body of work produced and published immediately after the war, either by or on behalf of the surviving members of the ZOB. These survivors recognized the importance of documentation and in their record of events it was inevitable that they would emphasize their own role in the uprising. These records were eagerly received by the Jews in Israel, and the controlling Labor-Zionist party which was in sympathy with the political ideals of the ZOB was happy to portray them as the real 'heroes' of the uprising, sidelining the role played by the Revisionist ZZW. In fact most of the ZZW fighters were killed during the uprising in the ghetto and few written records were made of their contribution. Revisionist leaders who returned to Palestine were preoccupied with fighting the British, forming an underground movement which was not involved in Israeli politics. As was the case with Masada, the emerging Jewish state needed stories of action and heroism with which young people could identify. It would have been reluctant to include members of a right-wing, previously Fascist sympathizing organization amongst the heroes who fought against Hitler, even if accounts of their bravery had been readily available. Even in 1977 when the right-wing Likud party under Menachem Begin took control of the government, little was done to make the Israeli people aware of the role played by the ZZW fighters in the Warsaw ghetto. A possible reason for this is that Begin had been a leader of the Revisionist youth movement Betar, but fled Poland at the outbreak of war hoping to reach Palestine. Instead he was arrested by the Soviets in Lithuania and was 'plagued by guilt for leaving Warsaw' and not returning to fight in the ghetto. As Libionka and Weinbaum suggest 'he may not have been especially eager to draw attention to the heroism of his party comrades who remained behind'.[31]

Like the stories of Masada and Nowogrodek, the story of the fighters of the Warsaw ghetto has been used to fulfill the requirements of a particular society at a particular time in history. People need stories of heroism with which they can identify and the 'hero' must be someone who complies with an individual's view of what is the right way to live and behave in a given situation. For the young people in post-war Israel who knew little of the many acts of resistance carried out by the Jews in Europe, heroes were those who took up arms against their persecutors, not those who went seemingly passively to the concentration camps.

After the destruction of the Warsaw ghetto and the transportation of thousands of Jews to Treblinka and Birkenau, people began to realize that the stories of resettlement were false and more determined attempts at resistance were made both on the way to and actually within the concentration camps. A few months before the storming of the ghetto, Ringelblum, describing the mood of the people, says

> Most of the populace is set on resistance. It seems to me that people will no longer go to the slaughter like lambs. They want the enemy to pay dearly for their lives. They'll fling themselves at them with knives, staves, coal gas. They'll permit no more blockades. They'll not allow themselves to be seized in the street, for they know that work camp means death these days. And they want to die at home, not in a strange place.[32]

Some Jews who managed to escape from the ghettos joined other resistance movements in Eastern Europe and formed guerilla partisan groups living in the forests, planning attacks on German supply trains and sabotaging railway lines and factories. These partisans obviously displayed considerable courage but only a few survived, often being betrayed by local populations or being hunted down and shot by Nazi troops. Many young people, however, even when presented with an opportunity of escape to the forests, decided to remain with their families in the ghettos. Zivia Lubetkin, who later gave evidence at the Eichman trial, said 'it is our duty to stay with our people until the very end' and 'to share the same fate' as those who are unable to escape. Another girl, Matilda Bandet, when asked by her friends to escape with them from the ghetto, said 'My place is with my parents. They need me. They are old. They have no means of defending themselves. If I leave them, they will be alone. I will stay here, with them.' Bandet was later to die with her parents in Belzec concentration camp. Her decision to remain with her family, knowing the fate that most probably awaited them, required as much courage and bravery as that shown by those who fled to become partisans.

Even within the concentration camps attempts were made to resist, to die with honor rather than in the gas chambers, but resistance required a certain amount of physical strength and mental determination, characteristics which the bodies of starving people close to death would be totally incapable of displaying. In the words of one survivor,

> The days and nights dragged on in the most terrible vale of tears ever conceived by man. Death stalked Treblinka without respite. People fell like flies, from sickness, from bullets, from the axe . . . everyone knew that if not today then tomorrow would be his turn. A majority of the prisoners became so depressed that their will to escape became paralyzed. But there were a few who maintained hope and made plans to save themselves'.[33]

In August 1943, shortly before Treblinka was dismantled, some prisoners broke into the camp arsenal and managed to push grenades, rifles and revolvers through a window and hide them under rubble. Another group of Jews had added petrol to the camp disinfector which they were responsible for operating, and later in the day the buildings were ignited, destroying the arsenal and many of the camp buildings. The chief guard and fifteen others were shot and more than one hundred and fifty Jewish workers escaped. Some of the escapees were hunted down and shot but some did manage to escape. In retribution, all the remaining Jewish workers in the camp were killed. Those who organized this revolt were members of the Sonderkommando, Jewish prisoners who were forced to work in the camp and assist in the removal of bodies from the gas chambers. They were mainly young, healthy men who received slightly better food and living conditions for carrying out this work but were under constant threat of death if they did not obey orders. Despite this they demonstrated considerable courage in organizing the uprising at Treblinka, and in October 1944 the Sonderkommando Jews at Birkenau, believing they were about to be killed before the closure of the camp, showed similar bravery in an uprising against the camp guards. They attacked the SS men who were attempting to organize a roll-call, with axes, picks and crow-bars and then before SS reinforcements arrived with machine guns and grenades, some men managed to set fire to the straw mattresses in the barracks, the fire rapidly spreading to one of the crematoria. Some prisoners managed to escape across the wire but most were caught and shot. A further two hundred men of the Sonderkommando were shot in the camp in reprisal.[34]

Despite the bravery shown by many members of the Sonderkommando they were regarded negatively by most Holocaust survivors and even seen as collaborators.[35] At Birkenau, one Greek Jew working at Crematorium II, explained his desire to remain alive, however unlikely that might be, with the words 'I have wanted to live through it . . . to take a revenge for the death of my father, my mother, my beloved sister Nella'.[36] However, despite the Israeli Jews desire for heroic role models in the post-war years, they had to be the 'right sort' of heroes, and like the ZZW fighters in the Warsaw ghetto, the Sonderkommando Jews who fought bravely with weapons in their hands did not fit this criterion.

Supporters of the Masada myth in the years immediately following the Holocaust preferred to believe that the Masada Jews died fighting rather than in an act of communal suicide. The question of whether suicide can in itself be considered an act of resistance or so-called heroism acquires considerable importance in the final years of the Holocaust. The belief that suicide is an act of weakness is belied by the actions of the small group of resistors remaining in the Warsaw ghetto after its destruction in May 1943. They had planned to fight the invading Germans face-to-face but when the ghetto was set on fire, one of the fighters, Zivia Lubetkin, recalls their despair, 'We were bewildered and lost . . . How terrible was this feeling of helplessness! How grave the responsibility we felt as the last desperate Hebrew warriors! We could not hold out for against the Germans' consuming fire for long without water or food or weapons'.[37] On May 8 the Germans began to send gas into the bunker where they were hiding and Lubetkin later recalled:

> Aryeh Wilner was the first to cry out: 'Come, let us destroy ourselves. Let's not fall into their hands alive.' The suicides began. Pistols jammed and the owners begged their friends to kill them. But no one dared to take the life of a comrade. Lutek Rotblatt fired four shots at his mother but, wounded and bleeding she still moved. Then someone discovered a hidden exit, but only a few succeeded in getting out this way. The others slowly suffocated in the gas.[38]

There is a reminder in these words of the Masada Jews who chose death rather than allowing the enemy the satisfaction of destroying them. In the last few years of the war many Jews chose to die as they could not face the burden of guilt they would have to carry for remaining alive when so many others had died. Lubetkin records the death of 'seventeen-year-old Frania Beatus, who had helped to smuggle Jewish fighters out of the ghetto through the sewers' and 'committed suicide on May 12'.[39]

A particular demonstration of suicide as an act of bravery and resistance rather than the coward's way out is shown by the suicide of Shmuel Zygielbojm, a member of the Jewish Council in Warsaw, who was sent to London in 1940 to publicize the fate of the Jews in Europe. In his suicide letter he says that he could not live 'when the remnant of the Jewish people in Poland, whom I represent, is being steadily annihilated'. He regrets that he has not been 'fortunate' enough to die with weapons in his hands, and concludes 'By my death, I wish to express my vigorous protest against the apathy with which the world regards and resigns itself to the slaughter of the Jewish people'.[40]

Resistance took many forms during the Holocaust, but it is evident that most acts of resistance would not have been classed as heroic by the founding members of the new Israeli state. As would later be the case with many Palestinians, after the expulsion of the PLO fighters from the camps in Lebanon in the 1980s, the word 'hero' could only be used to signify an armed fighter rising up against the oppressor. In both cases heroism implies physical action, a concept at odds with Ringelbaum's comment on the 'quiet, passive heroism of the common Jew'.

All nations have heroic myths, depicting courageous warrior heroes who are intended to serve as role models for each successive generation. For a newly formed nation intent on maintaining its borders it is essential that new myths are created depicting warrior heroes who fight and if necessary die in order to defend their nation and its people. This was particularly true for the new nation of Israel in the years following World War II. The Masada myth aimed to emphasize the heroism of first-century Jews in their struggle against the Romans, but for the newly formed Israeli state new 'heroes' were needed who demonstrated the same fighting spirit but who also shared the political and social ideals of the founders of the new state. One such 'hero' around whom a heroic myth was created was the young parachutist, Hannah Szenes, who was part of a group of *Yishuv* volunteers who were sent to Eastern Europe in 1944 to work with the British army, primarily to make contact with Allied pilots trapped in enemy territory and assist them in getting back, but also to contact Jewish communities and encourage the formation of Zionist movements. Before being able to undertake her mission, Szenes was captured as she crossed the border into Hungary, tortured, tried and convicted of treason and executed on November 7, 1944, 'refusing a blindfold in order to face her

firing squad'.[41] Szenes was a Hungarian Jew who joined a
Zionist youth group in Budapest and emigrated to pre-state
Israel in 1939, becoming a member of a *kibbutz*. Other members
of the group were captured and killed, including Haviva Reik
and Rafael Reiss who were shot in a forest in Slovakia together
with two hundred and fifty Jewish prisoners, the bodies being
thrown into a mass grave. Peretz Goldstein was shot in
Mauthausen concentration camp and the oldest member of the
group Enzo Sereni was killed in Dachau. Although these parachutists are remembered in Israel it is Hannah Szenes who
achieved the status of 'Zionist hero', receiving a full state
funeral in1948 immediately after the War of Independence.
The reasons for this and the processes involved in constructing
a heroic myth around this undoubtedly courageous young
woman have been analyzed by Judith Baumel-Schwartz in her
book *Perfect Heroes*, in which she reveals the importance of
myth in forming a national collective memory.[42]

Yael Zerubavel has commented on the 'dual classification'
operating in the 1940s, which defined 'armed resistance to the
Nazis as "heroic"' but the death of millions in the concentration camps as "nonheroic".[43] Although several of the
parachutists did die alongside European Jews in the Holocaust
they were commemorated in post-war Israel as heroic representatives of the *Yishuv*, and the Holocaust was rarely
mentioned in commemoration ceremonies. In Baumel-
Schwartz's words they were 'no longer simple volunteers but
envoys of the Yishuv's elite who came to save their brethren.
Those killed in the line of duty underwent a transformation
from brave parachutists to symbols of Israeli heroism'.[44] The
parachutists themselves, most of whom failed to complete
their mission, did not consider themselves to be "heroes", as
one of them wrote in a letter to his wife, "Please don't let them
make me a national hero because this wasn't heroism. Only
here did I see just how much too weak we are to be called
heroes".[45]

Hannah Szenes, who was tortured and shot by the Nazi
supporting Hungarian security services, became the perfect
hero for the new state emerging after the War of
Independence, a war in which thousands of young fighters

had lost their lives. Her Hungarian background was down-played and her embrace of Zionism and migration to Palestine emphasized. Baumel-Schwartz points to the 'romantic aspect' of Szenes' story in which

> her youth, her passionate temperament, and the fact that she had no romantic involvement with men brought to mind the persona of another fighter, namely, Joan of Arc, who, like Szenes, engaged in a heroic struggle to rescue her people. Thus, the myth was born of an unsullied virgin who sacrifices her life for her mission and chooses to die rather than to submit to personal and national disgrace.[46]

Szenes could be linked in commemoration with the young fighters who had died fighting for independence rather than with the Jews of the diaspora who had seemingly meekly accepted their fate. Her youth and consequent lack of a past history meant that she could be transformed into a symbolic national hero, endowed with the qualities required of such a hero while at the same time ignoring any aspects of her life or mission which did not conform with this image. The fact that the parachutists' mission was organized by British secret serv-ices together with the Jewish Agency was downplayed, and was portrayed as an operation carried out by Yishuv Jews with the aim of contacting Jewish communities in Nazi-occupied countries to encourage resistance and strengthen Zionist movements. In reality the British wished to recruit volunteers from Palestine to join British commando units as their European origins and knowledge of local languages made them particularly useful in gathering intelligence. They were encouraged to enlist in the British army to ensure their safety if captured and it was made clear that one of their main roles was to assist captured British soldiers to escape. The fact that Szenes was captured shortly after crossing the Hungarian border meant that she was unable to carry out her mission and although there is no doubt that she showed considerable courage and bravery there were many other courageous people engaged in similar missions who were not transformed into national heroes and given state funerals. Szenes was frequently referred to as a 'Zionist warrior' or 'anti-Fascist warrior' depending on the particular political allegiance of the speaker, but the use of the word warrior equates her with those who fought and died in battles for the Israeli state.[47] In reality she died as part of the Holocaust, enduring torture and death like so many other European Jews, with no opportunity for taking part in armed resistance. The image of Szenes as a warrior and an 'unsullied virgin', in other words as an Israeli Joan of Arc, began to be questioned in the decades following her death and in the 1990s when a collection of love letters written to her by a young Hungarian Jew was published she came to be seen as a normal young woman, enjoying life and eager for the opportunity for adventure which the mission she was to embark on provided.

Hannah Szenes was converted into a mythical hero suitable for the new Israeli state, and a group of Yishuv parachutists with whom she was associated also became part of the mythical heroic narrative required by the state.[48] The process by which this happened, outlined by Baumel-Schwartz, may be interpreted in the light of Roland Barthes's theory of myth formation in which a sign is converted into a secondary mythological signifier. In September 1944 a group of seven Slovakian parachutists proposing to enter Romania landed at Banska Bystrica airport in Slovakia, and before setting off on their mission were persuaded to have their photographs taken by a local soldier. All of these parachutists were killed while crossing Slovakia, including Haviva Reik and Rafael Reiss who as previously mentioned were shot and thrown into a mass grave. At the end of the war the photograph was found in a Prague museum and taken back to Palestine where it became widely reproduced. The photograph, like Barthes's picture of the black soldier saluting the French flag, acts as a signifier with the parachutists dressed in British officers' uniforms being the signified. Together they form a sign which is gradually transformed into a secondary mythological signifier. In the years immediately after the war the parachutists in the photograph were perceived as individual characters, but during the 1950s they came to represent a new sign or concept, that of anonymous 'heroic figures' who were prepared to fight and face death for the new Zionist state and who represented the ideals of that state.

The importance to a newly formed state of possessing such heroic figures who can be used as role-models for successive generations is obvious, but the desire for such figures can lead to a misinterpretation of history, and the word 'heroic' may come to signify a very narrow sphere of human activity desired by a particular state. Conversely, the mythical signifier 'hero' can be applied to many different concepts and consequently becomes meaningless. I have used the Holocaust and the reactions towards it by the emerging Israeli state to demonstrate the difficulties encountered when attempting to use the signifier 'hero' or 'heroic'. In most cases the behaviors signified by these words are not exceptional and may be demonstrated by most human beings placed in the same conditions. In other words so-called heroic behavior may be an essential part of human nature only needing the right conditions to become manifest. As I shall explore in detail later, the ability to demonstrate such behavior, whether it be active heroism or steadfastness, is determined by a large number of hereditary and environmental factors. These factors assume particular importance when considering the actions of the many non-Jews who assisted the Jews of Europe to escape capture and persecution during the Holocaust.

The story of Nicholas Winton and the rescue of Czech Jewish children from Prague prior to the Nazi invasion of Czechoslovakia in 1939 bears some resemblance to the story of Hannah Szenes and her fellow parachutists, the selection of one person from a group of equally courageous people to be celebrated as a 'heroic' national figure being a common factor. In the case of Nicholas Winton, however, this selection did not result from the desire to acquire a 'hero' who would serve as a role model for a newly formed nation, but rather from the actions of a few, mainly well-intentioned individuals who had their own reasons for transforming the one surviving member of a complex group operation carried out fifty years previously into a lauded and honored 'hero'. Winton himself was somewhat embarrassed by the attention and certainly did not consider himself to be a hero. In her book about her father's life, Barbara Winton describes how he was 'portrayed as a brave altruist who acted when others did nothing, putting himself in harm's way to single-handedly save a generation of Czech Jewish children. This story is not true' she says, 'at least not entirely true'. Continuing she explains how 'a myth has developed since 1988, which has become the truth as well as the defining episode of his life to many people'.[49] She believes that her father's character and his world outlook meant that he was the right person, in the right place at the right time, but that anyone else in the same situation and with the same strong feelings about an injustice would behave in the same way and try to make a difference.

Winton in fact spent only three weeks in Prague during January 1939, a few months before the German invasion. He was on his way to a skiing trip in Switzerland when his friend and fellow socialist, Martin Blake, persuaded him to go to Prague where Blake was working for the British Committee for Refugees from Czechoslovakia. In Prague Winton joined up with a group of mainly British people who were attempting to assist and where possible provide transport to Britain for refugees who had fled to Prague after the German occupation of the Sudetenland. As Anthony Grenville makes clear 'the key figure in the rescue of refugees from Czechoslovakia was Doreen Warriner, a young academic from University College London, who arrived in Prague in October 1938'.[50] Warriner set up an office in Prague, from where operations were organized with the initial aim of rescuing political refugees but also Jews who were fleeing from Nazi occupied territory. She liaised with workers in Britain to obtain visas and arranged for the transport of hundreds of refugees by train through Poland, personally accompanying them on a number of occasions. Grenville describes one of Warriner's 'most memorable exploits' which was to 'guide two groups of endangered women and children from Prague's railway stations to safe accommodation in cheap hotels and hostels, and this on the day after the German army entered Prague, when the streets were filled with German military units'.[51] Warriner only returned to Britain in April 1939 when the situation became too dangerous.

Warriner was concerned that she could not do more to help the children and was relieved when Nicholas Winton agreed to take over emigration requirements for Jewish children. He worked with various organizations on compiling lists of children and when he returned to England undertook the difficult task of finding sponsors and homes for the children, ably assisted in this by his mother. The organization of the refugee transports from the Czech end was taken over by Trevor Chadwick, a teacher from England, who had originally travelled to Prague to take two refugee boys back to his school in Dorset. He returned to work with Warriner, and together with another worker, Bill Barazetti, made all the arrangements for the emigration of the children 'whose entry to Britain had been secured by Winton in London', including organizing the trains which took them to Britain and accompanying them to the railway station in Prague under the watchful eye of German soldiers. He even managed to find a printer who could forge missing entry documents 'for the Germans to stamp so the train could leave'.[52] Grenville notes that Chadwick also arranged flights for Jewish children 'though these have not received any of the publicity accorded to the train transports'.[53] Chadwick returned to Britain in June 1939 'after seeing off a train transport with 123 children on board on 2 June'. Interestingly a memorial statue depicting Winton with two of the rescued children was unveiled in Prague's main railway station in September 2009 as part of the commemoration of the 70th anniversary of the last *Kindertransport* train. In reality it was Chadwick and not Winton who accompanied the children to the station.

In an article written by Monica Porter, the partner of Nicholas Winton's son Nick, in January 2011, entitled 'A Very Reluctant Hero', she quotes Winton as saying,

I ran the operation from London in my spare time, while working as a stockbroker in the city, and it took a lot of persistence and resolve – lobbying the Home Office for approval, enlisting the support of charities, religious organizations, refugees' aid groups and the press. But my associate Trevor Chadwick was in a trickier situation: he managed things at the

Prague end, organizing the children and the trains, and dealing with the Gestapo.[54]

There are many reasons why Nicholas Winton, just one of a group of courageous people working to rescue refugees from Czechoslovakia, was claimed as a national hero both in Britain and in the Czeck republic, named as 'Britain's Schindler', and portrayed as working single-handedly under constant threat, to rescue Jewish children. Winton constantly played down his own role and told Monica Porter, 'what I did wasn't heroic because I was never in danger. I took on a big task but did it from the safety of my home in Hampstead'. Porter says 'it is gracious of him to acknowledge this truth, but nobody is listening – least of all the hundreds of Czech *kinder* whom he saved from the Holocaust by bringing them to London in the nick of time and placing them with English foster families'.[55] Winton insisted that Warriner and Chadwick who stayed in Prague when conditions became dangerous were far more 'obvious candidates' for the appellation of 'British Schindler' than himself. He also acknowledged that one of the reasons why Chadwick had received so little recognition for his role in the *kindertransport* was that 'he died many years ago while I'm still here'.[56] Both Chadwick and Warriner died in the 1970s when most people who had been involved in the horrors of the war were trying to get on with their lives and forget the traumatic experiences of the past. By the 1980s many survivors became more willing to talk about their past and investigate the details of their early lives, and it was in 1988 that Winton's wife, Grete, found a bundle of papers in the attic of their home containing details of the rescued children. Realizing that this may be of historical interest she gave the scrapbook to Elisabeth Maxwell who was a Holocaust researcher and also the wife of Robert Maxwell, himself a Czechoslovakian born Jew who had escaped from the Nazis and who was the owner of the Mirror Group Newspapers. Maxwell published a three-page article on 'The Lost Children' in the *Sunday Mirror*, and Winton's story was then publicized on a popular television program called 'That's Life' presented by Esther Rantzen, with Winton invited to sit on the front row in the studio. Stephen

Moss who interviewed Winton in 2014, recalls that Winton 'was given no warning of what was to unfold and was not best pleased to have been tricked for the purpose of instant television drama – and bucketfuls of tears'.[57] The emotional drama which resulted when it was revealed that all members of the audience were survivors of the *kindertransport*, was obviously a coup for the producers and presenter of the program but it also proved to be the start of the myth which was to result in the conversion of a resourceful and caring man with a social conscience into a lauded Holocaust hero.

Contrary to most reports Winton had not kept his role in the *kindertransport* mission secret and his son Nick recalls that it was occasionally brought up in conversation 'at the dinner table'. He had in fact referred to this episode of his life in his election leaflet when he stood unsuccessfully for election to Maidenhead town council in 1954. Winton himself admits that 'what I did in those nine months of 1939 was only a small part of my life. I went on to do many other things afterwards, which were more important to me. That's why I didn't talk about it'. He adds 'I just wish some of these reporters would be more accurate, the problem is they don't always listen'.[58]

The question remains as to why Nicholas Winton was hailed as the 'hero' of the Czech *kindertransport* rescue when others who faced real danger in Prague were forgotten. The rescued children who were invited to appear on Esther Rantzen's program were then in their 60s and 70s, wanting answers about their past and information they could hand on to their grandchildren. They wanted someone they could thank for saving them from the gas chambers, and when Winton's role in the rescue was revealed they viewed him as their savior and idolized him. It was so much easier to focus on one living person as a 'hero' than a group of people who were now dead and who had received little recognition

Winton was young, adventurous, had a social conscience and hated injustice of any sort. He also came from a wealthy family who had many influential contacts in Britain, and because of their background were familiar with the situation in Czechoslovakia. The rescue of the Czech children was a task he could involve himself in while continuing to hold down a job as a stockbroker in the city. After the war he worked for the International Refugee Organization and the International bank for Reconstruction and Development, and in 1983 was awarded an MBE for working to establish the Abbeyfield homes for the elderly, all of which he considered to be more important than his contribution to the *kindertransport* operation. However, it was for this role that he was awarded a knighthood in 2003, and in 2010 was named a British Hero of the Holocaust by the British Government. Winton has also received many awards and honors from the Czech government, including, in October 2014, their highest honor, the Order of the White Lion, and he is honored there as a national hero 'afforded the sort of VIP treatment enjoyed mainly by Heads of State and Hollywood A-listers'.[59] Like Hannah Szenes in Israel, Winton has been transformed into a symbol of heroism, reinforcing the idea that amidst all the horrors that occurred in their country during Nazi occupation, there was at least one heroic figure, a symbol of hope, who could transform 'the pain of the Holocaust' into 'uplifting messages of hope'.[60] It could be that the post-war leaders of Czechoslovakia, suffering from a collective guilt for agreeing with demands to cede the German speaking Sudetenland to Nazi Germany, were only too ready to hail as a hero someone who had played a part in rescuing Jewish children from the advancing German troops, and a real live hero was obviously preferable to those long dead.

Doreen Warriner wrote down her recollections of her time in Prague when she was forced to leave in April 1939 but as Susan Cohen writes 'it was not until 1972 that she seriously thought about writing a small book based on her factual account which she called 'Winter in Prague'.[61] One of her co-workers, Robert Stopford, who had been sent to Prague in October 1938 by the British Treasury and in the words of Anthony Grenville was 'one of the unsung heroes of the story' and 'instrumental in facilitating the entire rescue operation',[62] had been unable to find a publisher for his own memoirs, and in December 1972 Warriner died suddenly from a stroke and her memoir was never published. 'Winter in Prague' did however appear as an article in *The Slavonic and East European*

Review in April 1984,[63] and was a detailed account of the role played by Warriner and others in assisting and rescuing Czech refugees. For obvious reasons this did not reach a large audience, and by the time Winton's story came to light four years later seems to have been almost completely forgotten.

Trevor Chadwick, who, as Winton himself makes clear, was in a far more dangerous situation in remaining in Prague and continuing to organize the rescue operation after the arrival of the German army, received no recognition during his lifetime and indeed very little after his death in 1979. His son, William Chadwick, did write a book entitled *The Rescue of the Prague Refugees 1938–39*, describing the role played by his father, Warriner, Winton and Barazetti in the rescue. This book was published by Matador in 2010 but is now out of print and received little publicity, Winton by then having been lauded as the main 'hero' of the operation. Although regarding all the rescuers as equally courageous, William Chadwick notes in the Prologue to his book that,

> Some have not been given sufficient credit for what they achieved, some have been credited with slightly more than the facts might warrant. One has been given huge credit for the deeds of others.[64]

Newspaper editors and television program makers with an eye for a good story profited from the mythologizing of Nicholas Winton's story despite Winton's own protestations that there were other individuals who had put themselves in greater danger and were more deserving of the honors that were heaped upon him. None of the people who publicized Winton's story had bothered to investigate the true facts surrounding the Prague transports and this is particularly true of the Slovak film director Matej Minac, who made a film and two documentaries on Winton. Talking about Minac's documentary on the Czech *kindertransport* called 'Nicholas Winton: the Power of Good', Barbara Winton says 'Matej had based the whole story on Nicky, with hardly any mention of the other valiant participants who made the rescue possible'. She suggests that this was because of 'his excitement at finding a living rescuer willing and able to talk about this historical event', but this was meant to be a factual documentary not a fictional film and most of the people watching, including many survivors, accepted it as the truth.[65]

Barbara Winton says that one of the reasons for writing a biography of her father was to 'disentangle the real person from the myth of the one-dimensional 'hero' figure, and to point out where truth diverges from myth in the rescue story'. She hopes 'to demonstrate to those who feel great acts need a larger-than-life or 'special' personality to undertake them, that really it's possible for anyone who feels strongly about an injustice or a need to make a difference themselves'.[66] Many individuals and groups worked to rescue thousands of Jews from Nazi-occupied Europe, most of them working with the constant threat of discovery, capture and death and yet they remain relatively unknown. An American couple, Martha and Waitstill Sharp, members of the Unitarian church, volunteered to go to Czechoslovakia to assist refugees and used methods very similar to those of the British group. They provided food and shelter, contacted sponsors abroad, compiled lists of refugees, provided necessary documents and personally accompanied refugees across the border. They stayed in Prague until August 1939, avoiding the many Gestapo patrols and only left when they realized that their arrest was imminent. After the war they received little recognition and it was only in 2006 that their daughter received a medal on their behalf at Yad Vashem where they were named 'Righteous Among the Nations'.

It does appear that a combination of factors resulted in the singling out of Nicholas Winton, a good, caring and resourceful man, as a Holocaust 'hero', one of the most significant being that he was still alive when interest in the Holocaust was at its height, and like Hannah Szenes could act as a mythological signifier representing the idea of a heroic Holocaust figure. The fact that he was of Jewish descent may have been a contributory factor, helping to counteract the false belief held by some Jewish people after the war that European Jews contributed in some way to their own destruction.

Tim Cole, in his book *Selling the Holocaust*,[67] considers how

Americans in particular have attempted to cover up the horrors of the Holocaust with feel-good myths, turning the Holocaust itself into a myth divorced from the reality of six million murdered Jews. He considers that stories of heroism and goodness are used by the media to hide the brutal reality and horror of the Holocaust. He criticizes Spielberg's film *Schindler's List* for emphasizing the goodness of Schindler himself and the feel-good ending for the Jewish survivors. The same criticism could be made of the films Matej Minac made about Nicholas Winton, and it is significant that his documentary is subtitled 'The Power of Good'. Perhaps it is inevitable that people would prefer to hear about heroes who they believe can overcome evil than be confronted with the evil itself.

THREE

Myth, Power and the "Heroic" Leader

Prior to the twentieth century the word 'hero' was more likely to signify an individual well known for their achievements and leadership on the battlefield or in politics than an unknown individual displaying courage or selflessness. In 1822, in his *Philosophy of History*, Hegel described men who 'may be called Heroes', whose actions do not arise from 'the calm, regular course of things, sanctioned by the existing order; but from a concealed fount . . . from that inner Spirit, still hidden beneath the surface'.[1] Such men, and they were nearly always men, were later to be referred to by Thomas Carlyle as 'Great Men' who were able to influence the course of history, but these men were not necessarily morally worthy and rarely altruistic, often exerting tyrannical power over others. The idea of the 'Great Man' is very much a nineteenth-century concept but was not universally accepted by thinkers of the time. The polymath, Herbert Spencer, a supporter of Darwin's theory of evolution, considered that so-called great men did not spontaneously arise in society but were actually a product of that society, and in his *Study of Sociology* writes: 'the genesis of the great man depends on a long series of complex influences which has produced the race in which he appears, and the social state into which that race has slowly grown', and he concludes that the great man 'is powerless in the absence of the material and mental accumulations which his society inherits from the past, and that he is powerless in the absence of the co-existing population, character, intelligence and social arrangements'.[2] In modern terms we can say that everyone is a product of genetic and environmental influences which may endow an individual with certain characteristics resulting in behavior which some may consider to be 'heroic'.

Perhaps the most notorious twentieth-century leader and the one least likely to be considered as heroic was Adolf Hitler. In the light of Spencer's thinking, Sidney Hook, writing in the middle of World War Two, asks, 'Was Hitler responsible for the anti-Semitic obsession of German Nazidom . . . or did the cultural environment and history of Germany make it obligatory upon Hitler to persecute the Jews'. Hook continues, 'a faithful Spencerian would have us believe that *both* Hitler and the persecution of the Jews could have been predicted from the state of German culture in the nineteenth century *and* from Hitler's hereditary antecedents'.[3] Hook firmly denies any such possibility but in the light of more recent scholarship and with a clearer understanding of nineteenth and early twentieth century German history it does indeed seem possible that given certain social, political and economic conditions a leader like Hitler would emerge, and that Germanic myths would play a large part in his emergence as a 'heroic' leader.

In the latter half of the nineteenth century various groups appeared in Germany in response to rapid industrialization and the perceived increase in materialism which was destroying traditional ways of life. These groups were collectively referred to as the *Völkisch* movement, the members of which shared a certain "essence", defined by George Mosse as '"nature" or "cosmos" or "mythos" . . . fused to man's innermost nature' and linking him to his natural surroundings.[4] This was a 'spiritual rootedness' relating the people to the ancient landscape in which they lived and to mythical heroes who had occupied the same landscape in the distant past. The idea of myth being a link between the 'cosmos' and human culture is very much in keeping with ideas developed by Carl Gustav Jung in the early years of the twentieth century. Jung's theory of the collective unconscious containing archetypes passed down from our earliest ancestors has been mainly discredited, but his thinking in the years leading up to the Second World War reveals the close connection he saw between *Völkisch* ideas and the current situation in Germany. Looking back on this time in 1946 he says,

... the tide that rose in the unconscious after the first World War was reflected in individual dreams, in the form of collective, mythological symbols which expressed primitivity, violence, cruelty: in short, all the powers of darkness. When such symbols occur in a large number of individuals and are not understood, they begin to draw these individuals together as if by magnetic force, and thus a mob is formed. Its leader will soon be found in the individual who has the least resistance, the least sense of responsibility and, because of his inferiority, the greatest will to power.[5]

Jung naturally had no wish to associate his own belief in 'collective, mythological symbols' with those representing the 'powers of darkness', and at a time when the horrors of Nazism were being revealed wanted to disassociate himself from the heroic myths of the *Völkisch* movement. However, in his Foreword to Jung's essays, Andrew Samuels notes that in 1934 Jung was writing that 'the leadership offered to Germany by the Nazis could develop into something positive, a kind of awakening of German potential locked up in the "German unconscious"'.[6] The influence of neopagan and *Völkisch* ideas on both Jung and the adherents of National Socialism in the 1930s cannot be denied and it is therefore important to examine the origin of these ideas in more detail, particularly the role of the 'heroic leader' who would be responsible for putting these ideas into practice.

Amongst the earliest written accounts of the Germanic peoples was that written by the Roman historian Tacitus in AD 98 with the title 'On the Origin and Geography of Germany', known as *Germania*. In addition to describing the geography of the area between the rivers Rhine and Elbe which the Romans had occupied between 12 BC and AD 6, Tacitus describes the customs and characteristics of the people belonging to the various tribes which had settled in the area. There is no evidence that Tacitus actually visited Germany himself and he was born forty years after the Roman army withdrew back across the Rhine in AD 16, consequently all information contained in *Germania* must have been obtained from written accounts made by those Romans who had been present or who had subsequently visited the area. It soon becomes evident that many of the comments made by Tacitus on the way of life of the Germanic tribes are colored by his own experiences of life in Rome under the rule of the emperor Domitian. Domitian's long reign of fifteen years came to an end shortly before Tacitus wrote *Germania*, and although he did introduce many reforms he was an autocratic leader who exerted strong control over the people and was disliked by the Senate. Tacitus saw Domitian as cruel, tyrannical and corrupt and in his description of life in Germany he does appear to be contrasting the freedom and strength of these people who were labeled barbarians with the life of those living in fear in Rome. Whatever his motives in writing *Germania*, this short account of a people living under constant threat of invasion by the Roman army remained relatively unknown and unread until its rediscovery in an Italian monastery in the fifteenth century. In subsequent years word of the discovery spread northwards from Italy and the words of Tacitus were appropriated by a people eager to achieve an identity and a unity in times when the threat of invasion or control by foreign powers was always present. Unfortunately passages of *Germania* were frequently misinterpreted and the context in which they were written misunderstood, resulting in the development of a myth which portrayed 'a glorious past' with 'an ancient people set in an equally ancient landscape . . . when the pure, unadulterated, heroic, and virtuous qualities of the Volk had been first thrust into history'.[7]

The progress of this myth has been examined in detail by the classicist Christopher Krebs,[8] tracing the idealization of their ancient ancestors by a German people controlled by the Holy Roman Empire and often under threat from the Turks to the east, to invasion by the French at the beginning of the nineteenth century and the later struggles for a united Germany free from outside influence. The same myth was adopted by the members of the *Völkisch* movement who reinterpreted the words of Tacitus in *Germania* to justify their belief in a pure race of German people linked to their supposed ancestors and the land in which they lived. The Italian cardinal, Piccolomini, who had spent many years travelling in northern Europe and was familiar with Tacitus' writing, played a large part in initiating the myth that the ancient Germans described by Tacitus and the Germans he had lived amongst in the middle of the fifteenth century were 'the same people at two different moments in history'. Krebs notes that 'this misconceived notion of an ethnical continuity would last into the twentieth century',[9] and that *Germania* would be used by various groups and individuals to further their own political ambitions. When Piccolomini wished to encourage the German people to join in war against the Turks he called on them to demonstrate the strength and bravery of their heroic ancestors, but when he wished to impress the Roman church in order to further his ambition to become Pope, he referred to the ancient Germans as 'a horde of illiterate, bestial brutes, vegetating in a primitive environment',[10] who were only civilized under the influence of the Roman church. The fact that the words of Tacitus could readily be used to support two opposing views of the ancient German people might indicate that Tacitus himself, while attempting to report accurately the accounts he read of those Romans who had taken part in the invasions was also eager to compare the simple lives and good customs of the German tribes with the lives of the Roman people under the corrupt and autocratic rule of Domitian.

Tacitus does commence *Germania* with the words,

> The Germans themselves, I am inclined to think, are natives of the soil and extremely little affected by immigration or friendly intercourse with other nations.[11]

He then proceeds to elaborate on his first statement, writing

> For myself I accept the view that the peoples of Germany have never been tainted by intermarriage with other peoples, and stand as a nation peculiar, pure and unique of its kind. Hence the physical type, if one may generalize at all about so vast a population, is everywhere the same – wild , blue eyes, reddish hair and huge frames that excel only in violent effort.[12]

He observes that the Germans 'take less than the normal pleasure' in silver and gold and that 'one may see among them silver vessels, which have been given as presents to their envoys and chiefs as lightly esteemed as earthenware' (*Germania*, 104).

He praises the skill and bravery of their warriors and in relation to the tribal leaders says 'it is their example rather than their authority that wins them special admiration' (106). He also praises the high respect the Germans have for women, 'a reverence untouched by flattery or any pretence of turning women into goddesses' (108). They seem to have a democratic system of lawmaking for 'on matters of minor importance only the chiefs debate, on major affairs the whole community' (109). Several direct comparisons are made to life in Rome such as the fact that 'the peoples of Germany never live in cities, and will not even have their houses set close together' (114), 'slaves in general are not allotted, as we allot them, to special duties in the establishment. Each has control of his own house and home' (121), and 'good morality is more effective in Germany than good laws in some places that we know' (117).

It is hardly surprising that many German people who read or were told of these words wished to return to the way of life of their ancestors as portrayed in *Germania* rather than living under the influence of the Holy Roman Empire. As Krebs says,

> Tacitus shone a bright candle into the dark, and its shadows mesmerized German eyes: Indigenous and pure, their ancestors had lived a hard but free, simple but moral life as tall, fair and flaxen-haired men and women of war.[13]

Except of course this was only half the picture presented by Tacitus and in most cases it was the half in which he was attempting to expose the faults of his own society by comparing it with a primitive, unsophisticated, tribal and by no means perfect society. Interspersed with the favorable comments are many passages in which Tacitus depicts the Germans in a very different light. The landscape which the *Völkisch* longed to identify with is described as being dreary and wet and 'either bristles with woods or festers with swamps' (*Germania*, 104). Their flocks 'are for the most part undersized. Even the cattle lack the splendid brows that are their natural glory' (104). Despite their 'huge frames' they have 'no corresponding power to endure hard work and exertion' (104), and 'when not engaged in warfare, they spend some little time in hunting, but more in idling, abandoned to sleep and gluttony. All the heroes and grim warriors dawdle their time away, while the care of house, hearth and fields is left to the women, old men and weaklings of the family' (113). The men live for war and 'have no taste for peace', often deliberately seeking out other tribes, 'where some war is afoot' (112).

Krebs notes how in the second half of the fifteenth century the German Humanists 'embraced the *Germania* as a belated gift from Rome, a truly "golden booklet"'[14] which portrayed their ancestors as pure and free, but to maintain this idealistic image it became necessary for certain passages to be ignored or even in some cases to be rewritten. Krebs describes a particular change in the text made by the German humanist, known as Celtis. Tacitus writes, 'Above all gods they worship Mercury, and count it no sin to win his favor on certain days by human sacrifices' (*Germania*, 108). Celtis changes the last two words to 'his sacrifices', which in fact makes no sense, but avoids accepting the fact that the German ancestors indulged in such a barbaric practice as human sacrifice.[15]

The German people had discovered ancient ancestors to whom they could relate, but what was now needed was a hero who would inspire people to fight for unity and independence. Such a hero was found in the *Annals*, one of Tacitus' historical works written about fifteen years after *Germania*, in which he gives a detailed description of events in the Roman Empire after the death of the emperor Augustus. As with *Germania*, the *Annals* remained relatively unknown until it was rediscovered in 1515. The first mention of Arminius, the man who for more than four hundred years would be regarded as the great German hero, is made in Book One of the Annals, which Tacitus begins by saying that he is going to 'relate a few facts' about the last years of

Augustus's reign. Augustus died in AD 14 and it was in AD 9 that the Roman army under the command of Varus suffered a humiliating defeat at the hands of a combined army of German tribes commanded by Arminius, a chieftain of the Cherusci tribe. Arminius had served as a Germanic officer under Varus and had Roman citizenship and a Roman military education, but persuaded other German tribes to join with him to defeat the Roman army. In the ensuing battle, which became known as the battle of the Teutoburg Forest, three Roman legions were wiped out and the Romans were forced to retreat. Varus was killed during the battle, probably by falling on his own sword rather than facing capture by the Germanic tribes. Looking back on their defeat, Tacitus describes Arminius as 'the disturber of Germany' and 'famous for treachery', a view shared by some of his fellow tribesmen who remained loyal to the Roman occupiers. Arminius's own father-in-law, Segestes, explained his loyalty to Rome as being 'not from hatred of my fatherland . . . but because I held that Romans and Germans have the same interests, and that peace is better than war'. Furious at these words, Arminius demands 'war against Caesar', saying to his fellow Cherusci, 'if you prefer your fatherland, your ancestors, your ancient life to tyrants and to new colonies, follow as your leader Arminius to glory and to freedom rather than Segestes to "ignominious servitude"'.[16]

Tacitus describes how Germanicus, the nephew of Tiberius, longs to avenge the death of Varus and how in AD 14 he is appointed to command eight legions to cross the Rhine and engage the German tribes in battle. The Romans follow Arminius and his men through forests and swamps engaging in many fierce confrontations, and eventually Arminius flees from the battle leaving his followers to be slaughtered. Determined to destroy Arminius, Germanicus returns to the lands north of the Rhine and as the Romans and the Cherusci confront each other Arminius asks Germanicus if he can speak with his brother Flavius who is fighting with them. Flavius describes how well he has been treated by the Romans, being rewarded for his bravery with money and gifts, but Arminius jeers at such a 'paltry recompense for slavery'. He speaks of 'the claims of fatherland, of ancestral freedom, of the gods of the homes of Germany' and condemns Flavius as a deserter. In the battle which followed the Cherusci, although fighting bravely, were eventually defeated by a superior Roman army.[17]

The hope that peace would follow, with the German tribes united after the withdrawal of the Roman army, was not fulfilled; instead, as Tacitus recorded in the *Annals*, after the departure of the Romans the tribes started to fight amongst themselves for supremacy in the region, with Arminius fighting to achieve power over the tribes. His ambitions eventually led to his death at the hands of one of his own tribesmen, eager to prevent one leader having too much power.

In the sixteenth century Arminius was given the German name Hermann by the Protestant reformer Martin Luther, and German supporters of the Reformation were happy to accept as a hero someone who had fought against Roman occupation just as they were opposed to the influence exerted by the Roman church. Arminius was seen as the German warrior who had been responsible for ending Roman expansion in Northern Europe and had fought selflessly to preserve German national identity. However, even if all the facts concerning the life of Arminius recorded by Tacitus in the *Annals* are correct, there are many reasons to question the accuracy of the myth which developed from the sixteenth century onwards and led to his adoption as a German nationalist hero in the nineteenth century.

Arminius did not in fact succeed in uniting the various tribes which occupied the land between the Rhine and the Elbe, and of about fifty tribes he only succeeded in persuading five of them to join him in battle against the Roman army. In the years following the retreat of the Romans many of the Germanic tribes migrated out of Germany to Italy, Gaul, Spain and Britain and consequently the people described by Tacitus in *Germania* were not only the ancestors of modern Germans but also of large numbers of people throughout Europe.

Arminius did succeed in defeating the Romans in the Battle of the Teutoburg Forest but he was not responsible for driving the Romans permanently out of Germany, as myth might suggest. It is highly unlikely that the Romans would have wanted to advance further north into Germany as it would have been difficult to establish supply routes in these remote areas and the Rhine did form a natural boundary to their territory.

It is clear that German people living under the Holy Roman Empire would long to return to a time when their country was free from outside influence, when their pure bred ancestors courageously fought off invaders from outside and when heroes arose who could protect the people and fight for their fatherland. The creation of a heroic past based on a complex combination of historical facts and mythical invention frequently occurs when a state feels threatened by external or internal influences and needs to establish an independent identity. A useful comparison may be made between the myths created during the establishment of the State of Israel, as described in the previous chapter, and the myths created by the German people in the four hundred years following the rediscovery of the works of Tacitus in the sixteenth century. The myth created around events occurring at Masada in AD 75 when a group of Jews were facing an invading Roman army bears comparison with the myths created around events occurring in Germany in AD 9 when ancient German tribes under the command of Arminius similarly resisted the advance of an occupying Roman army. In both cases original records of the events were lost but later rediscovered, and new translations were often selective in their depiction of events, choosing to emphasize aspects that would appeal to an audience eager to reclaim a heroic past. In the early years of the establishment of the State of Israel the myth of Masada played a vital part in providing people with heroic ancestors, just as in the sixteenth and again in the nineteenth centuries nationalist movements in Germany identified with what they perceived as their heroic and pure bred ancestors.

Individual heroes were also important to serve as role models and as Hannah Szenes became the 'perfect hero' for the newly independent Israel so Arminius became the 'perfect hero' for nationalistic Germans. Both, of course, acted courageously, but in the creation of the heroic myth their stories became manipulated, with unwanted facts being ignored and certain incidents being embellished. Arminius, or Hermann, was turned into a symbol of the German people and in the seventeenth century a cult developed around him with operas and plays being written, in which he is cast in various heroic roles bearing little relation to the reality of his life. In these plays he comments on the current state of Germany, the corruption of the German language and foreign infiltration of German culture, or as Krebs comments 'how the "majestic, proper, pure and abundant mother tongue" has been subjected to the slavish existence of a "bastard" – bastardized not only by the French but also Italian and Latin words! Had he fought the Romans in vain after all?'[18]

The defeat of Napoleon and the end of the Holy Roman Empire at the beginning of the nineteenth century prompted a renewed interest in German language and literature and a rise in nationalism. Unification of Germany and the formation of the German Empire in 1871 was followed by rapid industrialization and urbanization resulting in the destruction of rural traditions and links with the past. Members of the increasing number of *Völkisch* groups wished to maintain these traditions and links to their native landscape where their ancestors had lived pure and simple lives. In 1873 a massive statue of Arminius was erected in the Teutoburg forest, becoming a popular focal point for nationalists and later a gathering place for assemblies of the National Socialist German workers' Party (NSDAP). Tacitus' *Germania* became popular once again, particular interest being shown in his comment that 'the peoples of Germany have never been tainted by intermarriage with other peoples, and stand out as a nation peculiar, pure and unique of its kind'. These words encouraged ideas of racial purity and led to the belief that 'the nature of the soul of a Volk is determined by the native landscape'. The idea of the importance of landscape encouraged views amongst some Germans that the Jews who were originally a desert people were a 'spiritually barren people', whereas the Germans 'living in the dark, mist-shrouded forests, are deep, mysterious, profound'.[19]

The *Völkisch* ideology was based on myth, not only the myth of the pure German ancestral race, but also later myths contained in the ancient sagas, the Norse Edda, and the German epic poem, the *Nibelungenlied*. These works contained stories of mythical heroes and heroines who had existed in a pre-Christian world, a world of magic, rituals and sun worship. The Poetic Edda of Iceland is thought to have originated in the ninth century but not recorded in written form until three centuries later. The *Nibelungenlied* originated in the Germany of the twelfth century but the stories it contains have much in common with those in the Edda. Siegfried, the hero of the *Nibelungenlied*, for example, is portrayed in the Edda as Sigurd the Dragonslayer. These stories were rewritten in modern German in the nineteenth century and their characters became very familiar to members of the *Völkisch* groups. As Mosse writes,

> As the ancient Germans represented people closer to the roots of the Völkisch tree than their modern counterparts, so the ancient religious beliefs, mythology and gods also came to represent the unfailing source of primeval strength and genuineness, qualities that were lacking in modern religious doctrine.[20]

Völkisch ideology appealed particularly to young people, partly due to the anti-materialistic, nationalistic views of school teachers and professors who impressed upon their students the importance of German history and culture. The German Youth Movement, an exclusively male organization, was founded in1901 in Berlin and spread rapidly throughout northern Germany. Their activities consisted mainly of hiking excursions in the countryside, singing around the camp fire and indulging in lengthy discussion sessions about 'Germanic faith, tradition, heroism, nature lore, and . . . the aesthetic qualities of Nordic man'.[21] Mosse describes how the leaders of many *Völkisch* groups dreamt of transforming their ideas into a political system that 'would revitalize the Volk and institute the appropriately Germanic form of government. At the centre of this vision stood the figure of a leader, a "strong man from above," one whose advent was inevitable'.[22] The idealistic young men of the German Youth Movement saw the outbreak of war in 1914 as the opportunity for which they had been waiting, when the true Germany would be reborn, and despite the horrors of the trenches the encounter with 'heroic military leaders' influenced the decision of many survivors to join groups opposed to the new Social Democratic Weimar government. The idea of 'heroic' leadership, as Ian Kershaw confirms, had long been 'a significant element in the ideas of the nationalist and *Völkisch* Right' and the 'heroic' leader was 'now envisaged in a man from the people whose qualities would embody struggle, conflict, the values of the trenches', and who would 'destroy the old privilege and class-ridden society and bring about a new beginning, uniting the people in an ethnically pure and socially harmonious 'national community'.[23]

In a speech given at a rally in 1927, Hitler's propagandist, Goebbels, stressed the importance attached by the National Socialists to the expression of their worldview 'in a way that can be understood by the masses' and referring to the *Völkisch* movement he says 'the *völkisch* idea has existed for 50 years. I will grant that it was stronger 50 years ago than it is today. But one must remember that on 9 November 1918 it was not this idea but another that triumphed. If the *völkisch* movement then had understood power and how to bring thousands out on the streets, it would have gained political power on 9 November 1918'.[24] In *Mein Kampf*, which Hitler wrote in 1924 during his period of imprisonment for leading a coup to overthrow the government and seize power in Munich, he clearly identifies himself with the ideals of the *Völkisch* movement, and establishes a direct connection between this movement and his own National Socialist German Workers' Party. He writes,

> the *völkisch* concept of the world recognizes that the primordial racial elements are of the greatest significance for mankind. In principle, the State is looked upon only as a means to an end and this end is the conservation of the racial characteristics of mankind. Therefore on the *völkisch* principle we cannot admit that one race is equal to another. By recognizing that they are different, the völkisch concept separates mankind into races of superior and inferior quality . . . And so it pays homage to the truth that the principle underlying all Nature's operations is the

aristocratic principle . . . Hence the folk concept of the world is in profound accord with Nature's will . . . [25]

Hitler was clearly seen by many as the 'heroic' leader for whom they had been waiting and although at the beginning of the 1920s this view was mainly held by members of the *Völkisch* Right, by the end of the decade it was coming to be 'the central, all-embracing idea in German political life'. The growing economic crisis and the seeming failure of the Weimar government to deal with this crisis led to the widespread acceptance of a leader who in his 'Appeal to the German People' in January 1933, delivered plans to reorganize the national economy, to 'preserve and defend the foundations on which the strength of our nation rests . . . bring back to our people the consciousness of its racial and political unity . . . base the education of German youth on respect for our great past and pride in our old traditions'.[26] These words indicate how *Völkisch* thought became incorporated into Hitler's National Socialism, although as Mosse points out, all supporters of *Völkisch* ideology were not necessarily Nazi supporters. In Mosse's words 'National Socialism was successful as a mass movement precisely because it was able to turn long-cherished myths and symbols to its own purpose . . . Adolf Hitler mixed traditional and acceptable *Völkisch* thought with his own brand of racism . . . '[27]

One particular 'myth and symbol' which appealed to the National Socialists was an engraving made by the painter Albrecht Dürer in 1513, entitled 'The Knight, Death and the Devil', depicting a man in armor riding a large black horse through a distinctively Germanic landscape. He gazes straight ahead ignoring two figures presumed to represent death and the devil who are watching him pass by. Many different interpretations have been attached to this picture but for members of the *Völkisch* movement the knight represented the heroic leader who, ignoring the dangers around him rides on courageously into the future, leading people into a new and better Germany. It is significant that this picture was much admired by the followers of Hitler in the nineteen twenties and thirties and in 1933, the mayor of Nuremberg presented Hitler with an original print of Dürer's engraving, describing Hitler as the 'knight without fear or blame, who as the Führer of the new German Reich, once again carried and multiplied the fame of the old city of Nuremberg to the whole world'.[28] Hitler obviously welcomed this comparison and in 1935 commissioned the painter Hubert Lanzinger to paint a portrait of himself 'as a medieval knight, astride a horse, wearing a look of determination as his gaze penetrated into the future'.[29] The knight of course, as Mosse points out, represented 'qualities usually ascribed to the ancient Germans – heroism, loyalty, honesty, racial purity', and so in embracing this image Hitler was also identifying himself with the German people described by Tacitus in *Germania.*

In 1924, when Hitler was in prison writing *Mein Kampf*, two other National Socialist sympathizers were finding themselves to be in sympathy with *Völkisch* ideas and particularly with the work which they perceived to be the source of many of these ideas, Tacitus' *Germania*. Hans Günther, who was later to be appointed professor of Race Science at the University of Jena, wrote a book entitled *The Knight, Death and the Devil: A Heroic Thought*, which was published in 1924, and in which he equated the ancient German warriors with Dürer's knight. He considered the 'heroic warriors' described by Tacitus to be the 'true representatives of the Nordic race', and the *Germania* to be a work that revealed a 'moral attitude . . . so elevated that in the face of it we should fall silent'.[30]

It is recorded that during a train journey which he took in 1924, Heinrich Himmler, the future Reichsführer SS, read *Germania* for the first time and was greatly impressed by 'the glorious image of the loftiness, purity, and nobleness of our ancestors', noting down the words 'Thus shall we be again, or at least some among us'.[31] Himmler had long been interested in *Völkisch* beliefs, particularly in ideas of racial purity, and he also had a deep interest in occultism and neopagan ideas, an interest not shared by Hitler. At several points in *Mein Kampf* Hitler attempts to disassociate himself from those who 'keep harping on that far-off and forgotten nomenclature which belongs to the ancient German times and does not awaken any distinct association in our age . . . it is typical of such persons that they rant about ancient Teutonic heroes of the dim and distant ages, stone axes, battle spears and shields',[32] in other words the heroes described by Tacitus in *Germania*. It is well known that Hitler was an admirer of Hellenic culture, which he believed 'should be preserved for us in all its marvelous beauty',[33] and he admitted that 'at the time when our forefathers were producing stone troughs and clay pitchers . . . , the Greeks were building the Acropolis'.[34] In public, however, Hitler was happy to go along with *Völkisch* ideas which portrayed him as the true successor of Arminius, for in their misreading of Tacitus these contemporary devotees of *Germania* were dedicated to the idea of Aryan racial superiority, an idea which was to be the main driving force of Nazi policy. As Krebs points out, 'whatever Hitler's private thoughts about the hirsute barbarians . . . he knew what marching tune to play and how to stir Germanic sentiment'.[35]

The writings of Tacitus encouraged the people of nineteenth-century Germany to identify with their ancient ancestors who had defeated the invading Roman army, but at the beginning of the century there was also renewed interest amongst scholars in the *Nibelungenlied*, the collection of myths and legends dating from the twelfth century, containing stories of gods and heroes handed down orally from previous centuries. Hegel, writing in 1796, considered that the German people needed to rediscover their own mythology rather than the mythology of 'a nation whose climate, laws, culture, and interests are strange to us and whose history has no connection whatever with our own'.[36] Hegel was of course referring to the Christian imagery perpetuated by the Catholic church, but this imagery was so firmly embedded that even after the collapse of the Holy Roman empire most Germans found it difficult to identify with 'uniquely German heroes, myths and legends'.[37] The *Nibelungenlied* incorporated myths from the Old Norse *Edda* which told of the dragon-slayer Sigurd and his bride Brünhild, and in the words of Williamson, 'offered a sweeping epic in which greed, lust and treachery predominate and God is strangely absent'.[38] Sigurd was renamed Siegfried and his story, which was gradually adapted to accommodate more contemporary German values, became popular with those nationalistic Germans who would later become involved with the *Völkisch* movement. It was Richard Wagner who, in the words of Williamson, 'brought the gods and heroes of the German "national mythology" to life for a European public', when in the middle of the century he produced his massive musical and dramatic work *The Ring*.[39]

Opinion remains divided on the extent to which Hitler was influenced by the works of Wagner but there are undoubtedly certain themes in these operatic dramas which appealed to his nationalism and to his ideas of the heroic. He records in *Mein Kampf* that when he was twelve years old he 'attended a performance of *Lohengrin*, the first opera I had ever heard. I was fascinated at once. My youthful enthusiasm for the Bayreuth Master knew no limits. Again and again I was drawn to hear his operas'.[40] When he was fifteen he went to a perform-ance of Wagner's early opera *Rienzi*, which seems to have had a profound effect on him. Unlike the four operas of the later Ring Cycle, *Rienzi* is set in fourteenth-century Rome with no German associations and certainly no mythical gods or heroes from the *Nibelungenlied*. It is based on the life of Cola di Rienzi, a Tribune who leads a popular revolt against the ruling aris-tocracy, and although partly factual presents a highly romanticized version of Rienzi's life which was developed in the nineteenth century. Rienzi is portrayed as a great patriotic hero who wishes to restore the greatness and power of ancient Rome and unite a divided Italy, and it is easy to see why the young Adolf Hitler was attracted to this story aided of course by Wagner's powerful music. Albert Speer recalls in his diaries the words used by Hitler when he insisted on using the over-ture to *Rienzi* to open his party rallies in Nuremberg,

> At the age of twenty-four this man, an innkeeper's son, persuaded the Roman people to drive out the corrupt senate by reminding them of the magnificent past of the Roman Empire. Listening to this blessed music as a young man in the theatre at Linz, I had the vision that I too must someday succeed in uniting the German Empire and making it great once more.[41]

Hitler did in fact possess the original manuscript of the opera, which had been presented to him on his fiftieth birthday and is believed to have been with him in his bunker at the end of the war.

Most of Wagner's operas are retellings of medieval German legends often referring back to more ancient myths such as those found in the Eddas or to the legends of the knights of the Holy Grail. *Lohengrin* was inspired by an epic poem about the mythical Grail knight Lohengrin, *Parsifal* is based on a thirteenth-century epic poem about the Arthurian knight Parzival and the keepers of the Holy Grail, and *Tristan and Isolde* retells the medieval legend of Tristan and Iseult. However, it was in the four operas of the Ring Cycle that Wagner fully recreated the world of ancient Norse and Germanic mythology, the realm of Valhalla inhabited by the gods, the Niebelheim underworld inhabited by an ancient race of dwarves, and the human world represented most fully in the second opera in the cycle, *Die Walküre.*

In his book *The Ring of Truth*, Roger Scruton poses the question 'Why did Wagner scour the myths and the legends in this way . . . why not simply start again from the beginning, inventing the characters of both gods and heroes, and also the story that brought them together?'[42] Scruton finds a possible explanation in Wagner's early involvement with the nationalistic 'Young Germany' movement, the members of which rejected traditional religion, placed an emphasis on the 'pagan culture of Germany' and 'aimed to unite the German lands under a single democratic government'. He believes that for Wagner 'the gods and goblins of the *Ring* cycle . . . were ancestral voices, speaking of values and aspirations that the German people had to repossess as their own'.[43] Wagner did not believe that these mythical stories were literally true but that they symbolized 'human passions and states of character' which were in some way outside of history. This idea of 'an older form of knowledge . . . implanted in the unconscious memory of the Germans' is similar to Jung's idea of the collective unconscious, but is repudiated by Roland Barthes in his essay 'Myths Today'.[44] For Barthes myth is a 'system of communication' and must therefore originate within history. It is not too difficult to see how a secondary system of myth formation could be built up around the ancient stories depicted in Wagner's operas and how the visual 'signs' depicted in these operas could be used by an observer as a signifier for a new myth serving to naturalize current preoccupations. Many interpretations have been made of the depiction of the Nibelungs, Alberich and Mime in the *Ring*, and because of Wagner's acknowledged anti-Semitism it is presumed by many that these unpleasant characters were intended as Jewish caricatures and were in fact seen as such by members and supporters of Hitler's National Socialist party. As Scruton observes, 'not only did he become Hitler's favorite composer, but the Nazi caricature of the Jew was read back into Wagner's villains'.[45] Alberich was a character from the *Nibelungenlied* who guards the treasure of the Nibelungs and may in fact be seen as Wagner's warning against the accumulation of wealth and private property in order to achieve power over others, in other words the capitalist system. The Nibelung dwarf therefore becomes a signifier for whichever concept the observer wishes to attach to the sign presented to them in the opera.

In his 1997 book *Wagner's Hitler*, Joachim Köhler put forward what he later admitted to be the astounding accusation that 'Richard Wagner had, amongst others, inspired the persecution and extermination of the Jews in Hitler's Germany', lending credence to the Third Reich's anti-Semitism and leading ultimately to the Holocaust.[46] Seventeen years later, exhibiting considerable bravery as an academic, Köhler wrote an essay in the *Wagner Journal*, in which he revised his opinion on the nature of Wagner's anti-Semitism and admitted that it was the Wagner family and other aggressive anti-Semites who had exerted the strongest influence on Hitler long after Wagner's death.[47] Köhler describes how 'Wagner grew up within an ideological tradition in which Judaism and Jewishness constituted the diametrical opposite of Christianity . . . this had been a firmly held belief for centuries; Wagner did not invent it'. He explains how, after the Napoleonic Wars, 'pride in being German grew to the same extent as contempt for non-Germans: that is, the French above all, alongside the Jews'.[48] Wagner's main concern was the 'liberation of human beings, including the Jews, from their so-called 'curse'. The idea of torturing or killing human beings for the sake of this goal would have been foreign to him'.[49] Hitler's virulent anti-Semitism as expounded at great length in *Mein Kampf* is very different to the philosophical meanderings found in the anti-Semitic writings of Wagner. Hitler in fact rarely mentions Wagner's antipathy to Jews, and as Joseph Horowitz points out, his obsession with Wagner was mainly used 'to legitimize the Third Reich as an organic outgrowth of centuries of German culture and history. Wagner's operas stirred Hitler to envision reuniting the German Empire and restoring it to greatness'.[50] Hitler's response to the opera *Rienzi* does suggest that he was more influenced by Wagner's seemingly heroic characters and the emphasis on a heroic past, than he was on any anti-Semitic readings of the characters in the operas.

Perhaps the one Wagnerian hero Hitler most identified with was Parsifal, an innocent young man who is drawn to the castle where an order of Christian knights is guarding the Holy Grail. Amfortas, leader of the Grail Knights and guardian of the Holy Spear, was stabbed by the spear when Klingsor, the magician leader of a neighboring kingdom, forcibly took it from him and the wound will not heal leaving him weakened and putting the Grail at risk. After learning of this, Parsifal overcomes Klingsor's knights, retrieves the Holy Spear, and on making the sign of the cross with it, Klingsor's castle crumbles to the ground. After some years Parsifal returns to Amfortas with the Holy Spear with which he heals his wound, the Grail is once more unveiled and the community is revitalized under the leadership of Parsifal.

This very brief summary of the plot of *Parsifal* will hopefully suffice to explain the various interpretations which have been assigned to the opera and why it particularly appealed to Hitler and other members of the National Socialist Party. In the 1930s a Nazi propaganda poster was made in which Hitler was depicted as a Parsifal-like figure holding aloft in his right hand a Nazi flag, echoing illustrations made of Parsifal holding the Holy Spear, while light streams down from above. Behind the figure of Hitler at the bottom of the poster are a group of his followers raising their arms in salute and occupying the same position as the knights of the Holy Grail in depictions of the closing scene of the opera.[51] The image in this poster illustrates the process of myth formation in a manner similar to that described by Barthes in relation to the image of the black soldier saluting the French flag.[52] The poster and the image form a sign showing Hitler being acclaimed as the leader of the National Socialist Party, but for the observer familiar with Wagner's opera this sign becomes a secondary mythological signifier indicating that Hitler, like Parsifal, is a great hero, blessed by the light from above, who will save Germany from corruption by alien forces.

The Christian imagery in *Parsifal* appears to be obvious, the Holy Spear which pierced the side of Christ, the Holy Grail which converts wine into the blood of Christ, and the Christ-like figure of *Parsifal* himself, all contributing to the view that Wagner had left the mythology of the Eddas and *Nibelungenlied* and reverted to a Christian mythology which he had previously questioned. However, the Christian imagery in the opera has itself been questioned and various other inter-pretations have been attached to the story of Parsifal and the legend of the Holy Grail, interpretations which link the opera with German nationalism and anti-Semitism as reflected by the National Socialist poster of Hitler as Parsifal. Kinderman notes that long after Wagner's death 'the Bayreuth Circle regarded themselves as Knights of the Grail committed to promote a racist nationalist vision of Germanic self-realiza-tion',[53] and it was with this group that Hitler developed a close association. Parsifal was seen as the true Aryan knight and the blood of the Holy Grail as the true blood of the Aryan race which had become corrupted by the alien figure of Klingsor, who like Alberich and Mime in the *Ring* was interpreted as a Jewish stereotype. The use of Wagner's opera to promote the ideas of National Socialism is, in the words of William Kinderman, 'a chilling example of an ideological reduction of an artwork to serve a murderous totalitarian regime'.[54] There is no evidence that Wagner was incorporating racist theories or anti-Semitism into the opera and in fact the first perform-ance in Bayreuth in 1882 was conducted by a Jewish-born German conductor, Hermann Levi, although it is reported that

Wagner had unsuccessfully tried to persuade Levi to convert to Christianity before conducting the opera.

It is clear that Hitler and his fellow Nazis, under the influence of the Bayreuth Circle, chose to adhere to a particular interpretation of the mythical narrative contained within the opera, an interpretation which attributed to Wagner 'a vision of racial regeneration to be achieved through political means'.[55] Although the warrior-like Grail Knights may bear some similarity to Hitler's Storm Troopers, important messages conveyed in the opera stress the need for compassion and peace, qualities certainly not in keeping with Nazi ideology. Parsifal may have been regarded as the perfect Aryan hero who would replace the old order, but throughout the opera he plays a somewhat passive, non-violent role. The Holy Spear is not used as a weapon and the destruction of Klingsor's empire is brought about by a seemingly supernatural act rather than by violence. It seems that Hitler, with his preference for a simple, direct message, converted Parsifal into a hero who could be used to convey his own message of nationalistic racism. It is of interest that the Bayreuth festival program in 1924 contained a message 'urging heroic recruits "as Knights of the Grail to join the great German battle for liberation"'.[56]

In contrast to Parsifal, Siegfried the "hero" of the *Ring* cycle of operas, might be regarded as possessing more of those qualities desired in a true Aryan hero. Wagner based Siegfried on the character of the same name in the *Nibelungenlied*, and intended him to fulfill the role of the true Hegelian hero, who would bring a new world into being. Roger Scruton observes, 'Wagner was reading Hegel's *Philosophy of History* when he began the poem of *The Ring*, and at first conceived the work as the story of just such a hero, Siegfried, who was to usher in the new world of human freedom after the downfall of the gods'.[57] Here was a hero with whom Hitler could truly identify, a parentless young man, initially frustrated and aimless but eventually discovering a heroic task which he seemed to have been ordained to fulfill. For Siegfried this involved slaying a dragon, retrieving the hoard of gold stolen from the Rhinemaidens by the dwarf Alberich and subsequently used by Wotan to build Valhalla the home of the Gods, and eventually breaching the wall of fire surrounding Brünnhilde, the daughter of Wotan, a barrier which only a 'true hero' could overcome. Hitler perceived his heroic task as restoring the 'true' Germany by becoming a 'dragon-slayer', but this time the dragons were those he saw as the enemies of Germany who threatened to destroy the pure German race. Siegfried slays the dragon with the sword Nothung, which he has reforged from the pieces into which it was smashed during his father's final battle, and for Hitler the sword became a symbol of the new Reich which he would build from the shattered remains of the old Germany after defeat in the First World War. Siegfried's cry as he holds aloft the rebuilt sword, 'Nothung! Nothung! New and invigorated! I brought thee back to life!',[58] would resonate with Hitler as he rose to power in the 1930s.

There is, however, another side to the character of Siegfried which, as with Parsifal, Hitler refused to see or acknowledge. Although Wagner originally intended Siegfried to be the true Hegelian hero, he is in fact represented, at least initially, as being child-like, innocent and self-centered, performing heroic deeds for his own self-satisfaction. He is rude and hostile towards the Nibelung Mime who has brought him up after the death of his mother in childbirth, even though he is unaware of the fact that Mime intends to use him to obtain the stolen gold and ring. Roger Scruton summarises Siegfried as follows,

> In the end we just have to accept that Siegfried is what he appears to be: not the new man or the artist-hero; not the forger of a freer world or the fitting deposer of a superannuated god; but someone who never quite grows up, an adopted child who is unable to form secure attachments, and who exists fully as a person only by moments, when the armor of the belligerence falls away.[59]

Hitler, unable to see through the complexity of Wagner's portrayal of Siegfried, desires to turn himself into the dragon-slaying hero, ignoring the fact that Siegfried's apparent bravery results from his complete inability to feel fear, and the outwitting and slaying of the dragon is for him merely a game. Siegfried is led by a bird to the rock where Brünnhilde sleeps and overcoming the flames he fulfills the promise that she will only be woken by one who knows no fear. On seeing Brünnhilde's female form he feels fear for the first time and for the remainder of the opera performs no deeds that may be considered to be heroic. He leaves Brünnhilde to seek further adventures but before doing so places the golden ring he has retrieved from the dragon's cave on her finger. He arrives in the kingdom of the Gibichungs where Alberich's son, Hagen, is living, who, knowing that Brünnhilde has the ring tricks Siegfried into winning her as a bride for his half-bother Gunther. This is achieved with the use of a magic potion which causes Siegfried to forget his love for Brünnhilde and hand her over to Gunther, seizing the ring back and placing it on his own finger. Although this treachery is brought about as the result of a drug it is not something that would occur in the traditional hero story, for the 'alleged hero has become a tool in the skilful hands'[60] of others, and Siegfried comes to be seen, not as a hero, but as an ordinary, vulnerable human being, or in the somewhat pessimistic view of Scruton,

> in the course of their lives men regularly betray, abuse or demean their ideal of the feminine, in order to pursue their wayward appetites. What Siegfried does here in a single act the ordinary man accomplishes during a lifetime of compromise.[61]

In the last Act of Götterdämmerung when Siegfried is being lured to his death the Rhinemaidens approach him and demand the return of the ring, but Siegfried refuses. While out hunting, Hagen stabs him in the back and 'consequently, this hero does not die a worthy death in battle or in a fight against a monster, instead he is simply murdered from behind'.[62] Before he dies his memory of Brünnhilde returns and 'the buried Siegfried emerges in all his child-like wonder from the grave of his forgetfulness, and reclaims his only love'.[63] It is too late however for Siegfried to enact the role of hero by returning the ring to the Rhinemaidens and freeing the gods and the world from the curse of the ring. It is Brünnhilde who now fulfils this role taking the ring from Siegfried's finger and riding on her horse into his funeral pyre. As she dies she throws the ring into the water and it is finally returned to the Rhinemaidens.

Hitler presumably did not contemplate the possibility that Brünnhilde might be the true hero of the *Ring*, or as Alex Ross puts it 'the one who destroys the illusions of male egoism',[64] for in Nazi Germany the role of a woman was to be a mother and a housewife, to care for her husband and to produce children for the new Germany. As he did with Parsifal, Hitler selected a mythical hero with whom he could identify, and onto whom he could project his grandiose fantasies. The fact that this was not the hero created by Wagner in the *Ring* would be totally irrelevant to someone looking for a simple, uncomplicated image which could be used to manipulate those who attended his rallies, and who were familiar with mythical heroes from the *Nibelungenlied* and with *Völkisch* ideas of the heroic leader who would lead Germany back to greatness.

Ian Kershaw, in his book *The 'Hitler Myth'*, describes how 'the idea and image of a "Führer of the Germans" had . . . been moulded long before it was fitted to Hitler, and for years existed side by side with the growth of Nazism, without it being obvious to the protagonists of the need for 'heroic' leadership that Hitler himself was *the* leader for whom they had been waiting'. [65] The heroic leader would represent the will of the people and understand the history of the German people. He would be 'a figure of outstanding skill and political strength, decisive and bold in resolution, to whom his 'following' could look in admiration and devotion'.[66] By the mid-1930s it was perceived, even by those not belonging to the nationalist *Völkisch* right, that Adolf Hitler was the one person who would fulfill these requirements. Hitler understood the importance of myth to those wanting a return to old German values, and with defeat in the First World War and the ensuing economic crisis, he was only too ready to take on the role of 'heroic' leader. In the words of Williamson, 'in its Wagnerian or *Völkisch* guise myth offered a way of thinking about art, religion, and the nation that was particularly suited to the political fantasies of Hitler and the racist policies of the Nazi state'.[67]

Hitler could assume the guise of a Parsifal or a Siegfried knowing that the people would understand the significance of these mythical heroes, except of course that Hitler and his fellow Nazis had completely misunderstood Wagner's complex interpretation of these mythical and far from typically heroic characters.

Herbert Spencer's belief that a 'great man' is a product of his society and 'the material and mental accumulations which his society inherits from the past', appears to be supported by the choice of Hitler as Führer in 1930s Germany. However, although Hitler seemed to fit the peoples' idea of a 'heroic leader', it was his own background and psychological make-up which enabled him to prey upon the nationalistic sympathies of the crowd and gain their support for his extreme anti-Semitic policies. Various suggestions have been put forward to account for Hitler's extreme behavior, including diagnoses of psychopathic narcissism, megalomania and even schizophrenia, but perhaps the most interesting and useful analysis of the reasons for Hitler's rise to power is that made by Carl Gustav Jung.

One of the key concepts of Jung's thought is that of the 'shadow', the hidden, usually unconscious part of the personality which contains negative aspects not normally expressed but always present just below the surface. Jung considered that the significance of Hitler was that 'he symbolized something in every individual. He was the most prodigious personification of all human inferiorities . . . he represented the shadow, the inferior part of everybody's personality, in an overwhelming degree'.[68] Part of Hitler's shadow was the buried resentment and hatred he felt towards his tyrannical father who beat him with a whip when he was a child and left him with a feeling of powerlessness which according to Jung led to a massive 'will to power' later in his life. Jung also considered that the hatred built up towards his father contributed to Hitler's anti-Semitism, the feelings against his father which he was unable to openly acknowledge being directed towards the Jews. Feelings of inferiority and rejection led him to grasp power when the opportunity arose, presenting him with the fantasy that he alone could save Germany, and these grandiose fantasies were encouraged by the admiration and support he received from the people. Jung believed that the German people were unconsciously recognizing in Hitler their own shadow, their 'own worst danger', and yet he was unknowingly utilizing this shadow to obtain power with promises of a new world order. Although many would disagree with Jung's analysis of the reasons for Hitler's rise to power, comparisons can be made between Hitler's appeal as a heroic leader and the more general appeal exerted by so many supposedly 'heroic' figures whose actions in some way entitle them to be considered as 'heroes'. Maybe these people appeal to those hidden parts of our personality which unconsciously influence our behavior and usually prevent us from behaving in ways which might be considered as heroic.

Jung believed that the hero archetype was part of the collective unconscious, expressing itself in dreams, and he was particularly obsessed with the figure of Siegfried as represented by Wagner. His view of Siegfried as the typical archetypal hero was demolished as the result of a dream he had, long before Hitler's rise to power, in which he killed Siegfried. He dreamt that he was in 'a lonely, rocky mountain landscape' when he heard Siegfried's horn and felt at once that he had to kill him. 'Siegfried appeared high up on the crest of the mountain, in the first ray of the rising sun' and as he drove down the mountain, Jung, in his dream shot at him and Siegfried 'plunged down, struck dead'. When he awoke Jung felt a compulsion to understand the dream and he writes 'suddenly the meaning of the dream dawned on me. "Why, that is the problem that is being played out in the world." Siegfried, I thought, represents what the Germans want to achieve, heroically to impose their will, have their own way . . . the dream showed that the attitude embodied by Siegfried, the hero, no longer suited me. Therefore it had to be killed . . . my secret identity with Siegfried . . . and my heroic idealism had to be abandoned'.[69] The appearance of Siegfried in the rays of the rising sun recalls the cult of sun worship which was common amongst the German *Völkisch* movements and associated particularly with hero myths. It is evident that Wagner was well aware of this association when in his opera, the sun rises on the mountain top as Brünhilde is awoken by Siegfried and sings 'Hail to thee sun! Hail to thee light . . . Who is the hero who woke me'.[70] Siegfried is the sun god, a link to the ancient pagan myths and sun-worship rituals, some of which were re-adopted by the National Socialists in the 1920s and 30s, the designation of the summer solstice as a national holiday being a particular example. As Richard Noll points out the Nazi flag 'contained a red field that symbolized the purity of Aryan blood, at the centre of which was a white solar disc representing the sun . . . the symbol of God to many intoxicated by *völkisch* utopianism'.[71] Hitler's own obsession with Siegfried as the true Aryan hero blinds him to the fact that in this myth, the awakening of Brünhilde by the person she perceives as a hero is the last 'heroic' act he will perform. He subsequently deserts Brünhilde on her mountain top, sets off in search of adventure, ends up in the land of his enemies who make use of him to deceive Brünhilde into marrying Gunther and is then stabbed in the back by Hagen, a sequence of events which would not have formed part of a traditional mythical hero's journey.

A contemporary of Wagner, whose works were also misinterpreted by Hitler and by those who were striving to present him as the true 'heroic' leader of Germany, was Friedrich Nietzsche. It is believed that Hitler never actually read any of Nietzsche's works and was only eleven years old when Nietzsche died. However, a photograph exists of Hitler on a visit he made to the Nietzsche archives in Weimar in 1934, in which he is seen gazing thoughtfully at a bust of the great philosopher. Hitler's and his fellow Nazis' interest in Nietzsche was stimulated and encouraged by Nietzsche's sister Elisabeth, who was a great admirer of both Mussolini and Hitler, and who after her brother's death in 1900 edited his manuscripts and in some cases actually rewrote his words to give the impression that he would have supported the nationalistic and anti-Semitic ideology of Hitler and the National Socialists. As had happened with Wagner, a myth was built up around Nietzsche by those who had an interest in distorting his works to serve their own purposes, and as happens with myths many people believed in their veracity, a belief which still exists to some extent today.

Two aspects of Nietzsche's thought which were misinterpreted and then adopted by the National Socialists in their efforts to justify the role of Hitler as a strong and powerful leader, were his frequent references to 'the Will to Power' and his idea of the *Übermensch*, a word commonly but incorrectly translated as Superman, instead of more accurately as Overman or even 'beyond man'. In *Thus Spoke Zarathustra*, Zarathustra says to the people gathered in the town square 'I teach you the *Übermensch*. Man is something that should be overcome. What have you done to overcome him?'[72] Nietzsche was not referring to some superhero who would save the world or his country from anticipated disaster, and would have been horrified at the thought of his *Übermensch* being adopted by Hitler and the Nazis as the symbol of a master-race. The *Übermensch* who possesses 'Will to Power' is concerned with exerting power over oneself, not over others, 'personal *strength* rather than political power or power over other people . . . self-mastery, including self-discipline, self-criticism, even self-denial'.[73] Nietzsche's admiration of great warriors such as Caesar and Napoleon has been discussed in Chapter One, and as Robert Wicks points out, 'even though he was, in principle, sympathetic to warriors and military types, his conception of the warrior was more closely linked to idealized classical heroics, courage and daring, rather than to any soldiers who consider it their mundane business to massacre unarmed civilians'.[74]

Nietzsche condemned anti-Semitism on many occasions, and certainly in his later years showed no enthusiasm for German nationalism, many of his comments being distinctly anti-German. He mocks Wagner's 'delight in some ancient indigenous (so-called "national") existence' and his 'appropriation of old legends and songs in which learned prejudice had taught us to see something Germanic *par excellence* . . . '[75] His disillusionment with German culture accompanied a similar disillusionment with Wagner's music, and in *The Case of Wagner*, published in 1888, he declared the Wagnerian idea of the hero to be a sham, the hero only being raised to heroic status by the music which accompanies the drama. Scruton comments that according to Nietzsche a Wagnerian hero like Siegfried 'is not a hero at all but a decadent human being', and like Wagner's other characters needs 'to be unmasked, to be deprived of their mythic costumes and returned to the bourgeois context from which they have been lifted into legend'.[76] Interestingly these words might be applied to Hitler who saw Siegfried as a great Germanic hero. It seems reasonable to assume that if Hitler had read and understood the works of Nietzsche instead of accepting the distortions of others, he might have chosen an alternative title for the famous Nazi propaganda film of 1934, *The Triumph of the Will*, echoing as it does Nietzsche's 'Will to Power'. In Nietzsche's philosophy the true 'hero' or *Übermensch* does not desire to gain power over others but mastery over himself.

The use of the signifier 'hero' in relation to Adolf Hitler would seem to be totally unacceptable, but if it is accepted that the mythical signifier 'hero' can be applied to many different concepts, and that the notion of the 'hero' as being morally worthy is just one historical concept with no natural meaning, then it is legitimate to explore, as I have done in this chapter, how Hitler came to be accepted as the 'heroic' leader for whom the German people had been waiting. As Ian Kershaw writes, 'The roots of "heroic" leadership ideas in Germany extend deep into the nineteenth century, to the political notions and the mythical visions of Germanic leadership associated with the romantic-conservative strain of early *völkisch*-nationalist thought'.[77] I have shown how the roots of these ideas in fact extended far further back into history, to the occupation of ancient German lands by the Romans, incorporation into the Holy Roman Empire, the influence of the Roman church and its language and the later influence of French language and culture, all of which encouraged the rise of nationalistic *Völkisch* groups intent on returning to the way of life of their ancient Germanic ancestors. This could only be accomplished with the help of a strong leader who would embrace the idea of a culturally and racially pure Germany. Ian Kershaw quotes J.P. Stern as saying the 'heroic' image of Hitler was 'as much an image created by the masses as it was imposed on them',[78] and was built upon 'already existing values and mentalities . . . on to which the 'Hitler myth' could easily be imprinted'.[79] The idea of Hitler as 'heroic' leader was a myth, but the whole *Völkisch* movement and the nationalist movement to which it led were also based on myths, stories often based on historical events which were misinterpreted and elaborated to provide a picture of a glorious past inhabited by a pure race of German people and strong fearless heroes. The people of 1930s Germany did not get the 'heroic' leader they imagined, instead they were drawn under the spell of a leader interested in projecting his own distorted image, intent above all else on achieving personal power, with fantasies of grandeur arising from his own thwarted ambitions, and a desire to wreak revenge upon those he imagined were his and Germany's enemies.

FOUR

Extreme Altruism and the "Heroic Imagination"

In previous chapters I have shown how the mythical signifier 'hero' has been applied to many different concepts resulting in the production of many different signs, the Homeric warrior hero, the American patriotic hero, the soldier hero, the freedom fighter, the resister, the state-sanctioned hero and the heroic leader. One concept to which the signifier 'hero' has more recently been applied, and has for many people come to be the idea of the 'hero' with which they most readily identify, is that of the person who is ready to risk their own life for the sake of others. An organization very much involved with increasing awareness of this type of 'hero' is the Carnegie Hero Fund which was set up in America in 1904 by Andrew Carnegie and Silas Weir Mitchell with the aim of recognizing ordinary people who undertake extraordinary actions on behalf of others. Mitchell had made a study of what he called 'extreme altruism' and used the word 'hero' to describe someone, usually a civilian, who voluntarily risks their life while saving or attempting to save the life of another person. In the previous century, those designated as 'heroes' were predominantly military leaders who fought and often died for their country's honor, but one condition for the award of a Carnegie medal was that the recipient should be an ordinary civilian rather than part of an organization such as the army which expected its members to behave in a suitably 'heroic' manner. Becker and Eagly in their research paper of 2004 comment that the usual dictionary definitions of 'heroism' which emphasize 'courage and risk of one's life as well as nobility of purpose . . . do not clearly indicate that it is the conjunction of risk taking and service to a socially valued goal that yields heroic status'. They continue, 'people who take risks merely for pleasure or to attract attention, as in extreme sports are not deemed heroic, nor are people who serve valued social goals without risk to their own life or health'.[1] Becker and Eagly, along with the founders of the Carnegie Hero Fund, are obviously adopting their own definitions for the signifier 'hero', but for many people the great sportsperson who brings honor to their country, or the doctors and nurses working under extreme pressure in the British National Health Service also qualify to be signified as 'heroes'. The difficulties encountered in defining the word 'hero' and the fact that most people who use it, although having a vague feeling of what the word might signify, choose to adopt their own definitions to suit their own purposes, means that the signifier 'hero' becomes a true mythical signifier with no natural meaning.

Herbert Spencer, writing in *The Study of Sociology*, attempts to explain why people have a preoccupation with 'remarkable persons and their doings', attributing this to the handing down of stories about warriors and men of action from primitive societies to modern times, examples being Homer's stories of Greek warriors like Achilles, and stories of mythical heroes like Sigurd in the Old Norse *Edda*. Spencer believed that 'the lessons given to every civilized child tacitly imply . . . that throughout the past of the human race, the doings of conspicuous persons have been the only things worthy of remembrance'.[2] People do seem to need stories of courage and action and 'heroes' with whom they can identify. Jung believed that the hero archetype is part of a 'collective unconscious' which leads us to identify with heroic figures and unconsciously desire to be like them. Sigmund Freud believed that in fictional stories of 'heroes' we also identify with the 'hero' and although the 'hero' may die we live through his death and survive. This engenders the unconscious belief that we too can survive and in performing a 'heroic' action we act out the role of the fictional hero, believing that ultimately we shall survive. Freud actually described a 'hero complex' in which people are driven to act out the role of a 'hero' in order to receive recognition and a sense of self-worth.

The particular acts designated as heroic by the Carnegie Hero Fund were originally referred to by the fund's founder as 'extreme altruism'. Altruism in its more general form involves acting to increase the welfare of others, usually without involving risk to oneself, and much research has been carried out in an effort to determine how the evolutionary history of human beings may have resulted in the development of altruism. Common sense suggests that the process of natural selection would favor those individuals possessing genes which are most likely to ensure their own survival in a particular environment. The evolution of more general altruism depends on the fact that closely related members of the same group are likely to possess similar genes, and it would therefore be advantageous for an individual to act in a way that would ensure the survival of other members of the group as well as their own. However, if genes for 'extreme altruism' exist it is difficult to see how they would be selected for when the individual possessing them is likely to die as a result of their heroic action. Anthropological studies have shown that in hunter-gatherer societies frequent warfare occurred between competing groups and it is suggested that groups in which some members possessed genes which contributed to so-called 'heroic' behavior would be at a distinct advantage even though some of these 'heroes' might die in the fighting. Smirnov et al. have carried out research to demonstrate that 'extreme altruism' may have evolved in response to war, particularly if the warring groups were small and mortality in the defeated group was high.[3] Frequent warfare would favor the selection of genes responsible for 'heroic' behavior, even if they were only present in a few members of one of the warring groups. The actions of these 'heroes' would ensure that the rival group was defeated and their numbers so depleted that the successful group would be able to take over their territory and food supplies and have access to new mating partners thus increasing the success of the group. The genes responsible for 'heroic' behavior present in the surviving 'heroes' would therefore be passed on to new generations, increasing the frequency of these genes and ensuring the success of groups possessing them every time war occurred. The question arises as to how genes selected for as a result of group warfare in our remote ancestors might contribute to extreme altruism in the present. Of course, there is no such thing as a 'hero gene', rather a group of genes which contribute to the formation of 'emotional and cognitive responses that support "heroism"',[4] responses such as anger, aggression and physical responses which support action. These are similar to the *thumoidic* responses possessed by warriors like Achilles and are brought about by electrical nerve impulses or chemical molecules responding to instructions from the nervous system and working to ensure the chances of surviving in hostile environments. The fact that these responses increase the chances of survival means that the genes responsible for them have been selected for and passed on to successive generations. The possibility that these genes were selected as a result of warfare amongst our distant ancestors does not of course mean that the processes which they control are only relevant in war, although primitive instinctual responses are important in modern warfare. Rapid automatic action is a characteristic of many so-called 'heroic' actions, and recipients of the Carnegie Hero Fund medal often describe how their response was automatic rather than being the result of deliberation. One young student who rescued someone trapped in a car during a flood explained, 'I'm thankful I was able to act and not think about it', and a man who intervened when he witnessed a young girl being brutally attacked by a man with a knife in his hand said, 'I think it was just instinct. Kind of like my tendency, that nobody in my platoon is going to get attacked without me doing something'.[5] David Rand and Ziv Epstein have studied the importance of automatic, intuitive processes in cases of extreme altruism and have concluded that most so-called 'heroic' acts are not carried out as a result of deliberative, rational thought processes arising from areas of the brain concerned with conscious action. Instead they are initiated by the fast, automatic unconscious parts of the brain responsible for many activities involving response to environmental stimuli. Rand and Epstein consider that there is competition between these two 'cognitive systems', one resulting in a fast, unthinking response and the other in a slower, controlled, rational response, the former being the characteristic response of extreme altruists or so-called 'heroes'. Their conclusions were made as a result of a study carried out with recipients of the Carnegie Hero Fund medal, in which they were asked to write statements describing their decision making. A control group were asked 'to write about a time in their life where either following their intuition or carefully reasoning through a problem led to a good outcome',[6] and from these statements twenty-five participants describing the use of intuition and twenty-five describing the use of deliberation, were selected. All three groups were then asked to rate randomly selected statements as involving either intuitive or deliberative decision making. The results showed that the decision making by the Carnegie group corresponded almost exactly with that of the intuitive control group, whereas there was virtually no correspondence with the deliberative controls. The conclusion made from the results of the study was that 'when extreme altruists explain why they decided to help, the cognitive processes they describe are overwhelmingly intuitive, automatic and fast'.[7] One problem arising from this study is the question of why a primitive response initially evolved as a response to a danger which might threaten the individual, is used by extreme altruists to protect or save another individual when this might result in their own death. It is worth quoting the response made by Rand and Epstein to this perceived anomaly. They suggest that 'extreme altruism may be a result of internalizing (and subsequently overgeneralizing) successful behavioral strategies from lower-stakes settings where cooperation is typically advantageous: helping others is usually in one's long-term self-interest in the context of most daily-life interactions . . . .This leads to the development of helping as an automatic default, which then sometimes gets applied in atypical settings where helping is extremely costly'.[8] This suggestion is useful when considering, for example, the behavior of those people who risked their lives to assist and rescue Jews in Europe during the Holocaust.

    An interesting development from the work of Rand and others in the field is that for many commentators an act of extreme altruism carried out automatically without active thought, is considered to be in some way more morally worthy than a deliberative act in which various possibilities are considered before action is taken. Risking one's life to save others has come to be seen as the extreme act of 'heroism', without considering whether rushing in to help might not always be the best course of action from a rational point of view.

The Carnegie type of 'hero' or extreme altruist does appear to be capable of carrying out actions that most people would be incapable of, or at least if faced with a similar situation would spend some time weighing up the pros and cons of taking action: for example the weak swimmer who sees a person drowning or the young mother with dependent children who is present at the scene of a house fire. It does appear that people who act automatically without prior thought do seem to share certain personality traits, and Andrea Kuszewski identifies these as being impulsive, argumentative, rebellious, ready to break rules and to challenge authority.[9] Kuszewski and others have suggested that this type of personality is shared with another group in society, certainly not considered to be 'heroic', namely sociopaths, and that there may actually be a genetic link between the two groups. Kuszewski lists personality traits present in both groups including low impulse control, high novelty-seeking needs, the ability to detach emotionally from situations and willingness to defy authority. Perhaps the most obvious trait separating the 'hero' from the sociopath is the seeming presence of empathy in the extreme altruist and the apparent inability of the sociopath to understand how another person feels. Kuszewski suggests that the difference between a person with extreme altruism and one with sociopathy 'could come down to the presence or absence of a few crucial regulatory mechanisms that affect expressed empathy'.[10] It is important to recognize, however, that Kuszewski's analysis is confined to the Carnegie type of 'hero', and that warrior 'heroes' like Chris Kyle, described in Chapter One, could certainly not be described as possessing large amounts of empathy, although he does seem to possess most of the traits of a sociopath.

The role of genes in the development of certain types of behavior patterns is a highly controversial subject but it is obvious that genes enhancing survival in hostile environments would be selected for during man's early evolution and that these genes are expressed in ways that do influence behavior, by controlling the production of chemicals and the functioning of neuron networks in the brain. A gene referred to as the MAO-A gene has been identified which affects the levels of serotonin in the brain and has been associated with an increase in aggressive behavior in some of those possessing it. However, there is some controversy as to whether this so-called 'warrior gene' is significant in producing seemingly psychopathic behavior.

Brain imaging studies have shown that people who demonstrate high amounts of empathy show increased activity in certain regions of the brain when shown pictures of people in distress, whereas people with sociopathic tendencies tend to have decreased activity in these regions which are normally involved with emotions and decision making.[11] Other studies have shown that people demonstrating altruistic behavior have higher levels of the hormone oxytocin in the brain, a hormone associated with social behavior and emotions.[12] However, it is important to recognize that the environment plays a large part in the development of personality traits and that the 'heroic' behavior of extreme altruists or the anti-social behavior of sociopaths may be the result of complex interactions between environmental stimuli and the development of neural circuits in the brain during early childhood.

The relative importance of genetic and environmental factors in the development of extreme altruism is particularly significant when considering whether 'heroic' characteristics are in any way gender specific. The work of Smirnov et al. suggests that genes for 'heroic' behavior were selected for as a result of frequent warfare between competing hunter-gatherer groups, and because it might be presumed that the fighters were male it is often also presumed that 'heroic' behavior is more likely to be found in males than in females. This is of course an inaccurate assumption for genes contributing to 'heroic' behavior would have been present in both sexes and the dominant role of men in warfare would be the result of male specific characteristics such as strength and body size, as well as societal factors such as the role of women in childcare. It is likely that the genes responsible for 'heroic' behavior were expressed in other ways in females, for example taking responsibility for other group members, making decisions on the best sites for food gathering and supporting the men in warfare.[13] Becker and Eagly have made an extensive study of the role of gender in 'heroic' behavior including a comparative study of recipients of the Carnegie Hero medal and those non-Jews who risked their lives to save Jews during the Holocaust. They found that up to April 2003 when the study was carried out only 8.9% of Carnegie Hero medal recipients had been women out of a total of 8,706 medalists.[14] They conclude that the male domination of this type of 'heroism', particularly in situations involving fires, potential drowning and violent crime is partly a result of the physical size and strength of the male interveners and also the fact that many of them had undergone some training in emergency situations, either in military service or as members of organizations such as the Scouts. It is also possible that androgen hormones like testosterone 'which some researchers have implicated' in the development of male aggression, 'also facilitate assertive physical intervention in risky situations'.[15] There is still some controversy over the role of testosterone in aggressive and impulsive behavior but more recent research has demonstrated that high levels of testosterone do activate nerve pathways in parts of the brain responsible for aggression. This response, however, is most obvious in lower animals, and in humans chemicals released from higher brain centers tend to inhibit the aggressive response.[16]

The other group examined by Becker and Eagly were 'The Righteous Among the Nations', that is the non-Jews who were responsible for saving the lives of many Jews during the Holocaust.[17] These rescuers certainly qualify as extreme altruists or 'heroes' under the Carnegie definition, as they risked their own lives attempting to save the lives of others. The results of the research indicated that slightly more women than men acted as rescuers of Jewish people in the European countries included in the study. Becker and Eagly make the point that one of the reasons put forward for the preponderance of males in the Carnegie hero group is that men are more willing to take risks than women. This supposition is not supported by the results of the Jewish rescuers study, as more than 20 percent of those who aided Jews were killed by the Nazis, a slightly higher percentage than those awarded the Carnegie medal posthumously. The importance of physical strength in many Carnegie type interventions was not usually relevant for those who intervened on behalf of Jews.

An extensive discussion of the factors that motivated non-Jews in Europe to help Jews threatened with Nazi persecution is made by Eva Fogelman in her book *Conscience and Courage*, which is based on personal interviews with surviving rescuers.[18] As a psychologist Fogelman is particularly interested in the personality traits of those who risked their lives and whether similar traits are found in all rescuers. Although, as with the Carnegie 'heroes', the actions of the Jewish rescuers sometimes involved an immediate, intuitive response to a situation, in the majority of cases their actions were well thought out and planned over a period of time, and in this sense did not conform with the idea of extreme altruism adopted by the Carnegie medal fund. However these were civilians who knowingly risked their lives 'while saving or attempting to save the life of another person' and it therefore seems that alternative explanations need to be provided for their behavior, in addition to the primitive, intuitive responses previously discussed. Fogelman writes of the 'ego gratification and self-satisfaction gained from successfully outwitting the authorities and protecting others', how the rescuers 'basked in the appreciation of their wards' and how many of them felt that 'this time of terror and mayhem was one of the most satisfying periods of their lives'.[19] Unconscious motivations obviously play a part in all so-called 'heroic' acts but Fogelman identifies certain motivational groupings into which rescuers may be placed, groupings which help to explain why some people became rescuers while others remained as bystanders.

The 'moral' rescuers were those who had a well defined sense of right and wrong and when asked why they reacted as they did, they often responded in a similar way to the Carnegie medal recipients, that they only did what anyone else would have done when faced with a life in danger. These people had been brought up to respect authority and do their duty and found it difficult to refuse when asked to help. They usually had strong ethical or religious beliefs even when this meant helping people of a different religion, and many of them showed high levels of empathy.

The second group identified by Fogelman were 'philosemites' or 'Judeophiles', that is people who had a love and respect for the Jewish people or individual Jews. Oskar Schindler, who Fogelman describes as a 'womanizer, a manipulator, and a seasoned briber', might be considered to belong to this group although his membership of the Nazi party meant that his chances of facing death were far lower than that of individual, small-scale rescuers. He was designated as one of The Righteous Among the Nations and considered by many to be a 'hero', but although he demonstrated extreme ingenuity and bravery and showed compassion for the Jews he saved from the concentration camps, it is difficult to place him in the same category as those rescuers who hid Jews in their own homes and lived under the constant threat of betrayal, discovery and execution. In many west European countries where anti- Semitic attitudes were not as prevalent, Jewish and non-Jewish people had played together as children, worked together and sometimes married each other.

A smaller group of rescuers were professional people such as nurses, doctors and social workers whose lives had been devoted to helping others regardless of their circumstances or their religion. Characteristically they were opposed to Nazi ideology and abiding by the ethical standards of their professions were ready to come to the aid of anyone suffering under the regime. Fogelman describes the case of a French psychiatrist, Adelaide Hautval, who 'refused to anesthetize prisoners for Nazi sterilization experiments', maintaining that 'such experiments were against her principles as a doctor'.[20] As a result of her stand she was deported to Auschwitz.

Many of these professional people formed themselves into groups or networks, thus increasing their ability to assist Jews in the areas where they operated.

Fogelman dismisses the idea that male rescuers were more likely to take part in 'heroic' actions than women, supporting the conclusions made by Becker and Eagly that women rescuers actually took slightly more risks than men when physical strength was not a factor. Like Kuszewski, she also identifies certain personality traits shared by rescuers, particularly 'having a personality inclined towards risk taking', special abilities relevant to the situation, willingness to defy authority, and the possession of a high degree of empathy. These are similar to the personality traits Kuszewski identifies in extreme altruists. As a result of her interviews with rescuers Fogelman noticed that the majority had spent their childhoods in 'nurturing, loving homes' with an altruistic parent or carer who taught them to be tolerant of other people's differences and encouraged the development of empathy. Although as discussed, the personality traits of extreme altruists are likely to be the result of their genetic make-up, it has also been shown that the childhood environment plays a large part in the expression of these genes, particularly in the development of empathy.

When the war ended most of the rescuers who had not fallen into the hands of the Nazis carried on with their lives and were certainly not hailed as 'heroes' by those amongst whom they lived. In Eastern Europe those known to have helped the Jews were treated with the same enmity and hostility as the few Jews who had survived the concentration camps. Anti-Semitism was the norm and many Jews and rescuers chose to emigrate to Israel or the United States rather than face constant threats and abuse. Although most rescuers admitted to feeling a sense of pride and self-satisfaction at what they had achieved, they tended to keep quiet about their wartime activities even within their own families. In countries like Holland and Denmark those who had taken great risks in hiding Jews from the Nazi occupiers were not generally recognized, often due to a sense of shame amongst the majority that they had not done more to help their Jewish neighbors. It was not until the trial of Adolf Eichmann in 1961 that evidence emerged from Jewish survivors of the brutalities they had experienced under the Nazis and also the role played by non-Jewish people in their survival. Many rescuers were reluctant to be hailed as 'heroes', claiming that 'during the war, they did only what needed to be done', in other words they were 'just human beings'.[21]

The idea that any human being endowed with a certain genetic make-up and a supportive and nurturing background is capable of performing an act of extreme altruism when placed in a situation where such action is required, seems to negate the idea that the people who perform these acts need to be awarded a particular signifier which raises them above other human beings. Maybe we are all 'heroes' just waiting for the opportunity to demonstrate our 'heroism'. This idea has been converted into a lifetime mission by the Stanford University professor of psychology, Philip Zimbardo, who devised the much criticized Stanford Prison Experiment in the early 1970s. He was much affected by the way in which a group of previously well adjusted students rapidly took on the role of prison guards which had been assigned to them in the Stanford experiment, behaving in a vicious and degrading way towards their 'prisoners'.[22] Perhaps wanting to compensate for his role in this experiment, Zimbardo suggested that just as people could be persuaded to behave in an 'evil' manner, they might also be persuaded to behave 'heroically'. In an article written with Zeno Franco in 2006 entitled 'The Banality of Heroism' he discusses his belief 'that heroic acts are something that anyone can perform, given the right mind-set and conditions'.[23] He wishes to debunk the 'myth' of the superhuman hero but considers that 'society needs to consider ways of fostering heroic imagination', for example by encouraging the young to read stories of ancient Greek mythical 'heroes' like Achilles, saying that although these stories are antiquated 'their instructions for the hero still hold up'.[24] Interestingly, as I have previously discussed, Socrates did not consider Achilles to be a suitable role model for the young particularly because of his 'possession of *thumos* untemperd by reason'.

Zimbardo and Franco admit that 'heroism' is not the same as altruism, which 'emphasizes selfless acts that assist others', but that it 'entails the potential for deeper personal sacrifice' and the commitment to a 'noble purpose'.[25] This 'noble purpose' does not need to involve dramatic action or physical peril and they use the term 'social heroism' to describe the act of standing up against social or political decisions we believe to be wrong. The 'hero' may be the 'extreme altruist' as defined by Rand or Kuszweski, or the soldier fighting in battle or the wartime resistor facing death or imprisonment, or anyone showing courage, fortitude or even compassion. By making everybody a possible 'hero' Zimbardo and Franco seem to be confirming that the characteristics they describe as being heroic are actually part of human nature, and shown to a greater or lesser degree by everyone depending on their genetic make-up, environmental background and the circumstances in which they find themselves.

The 2006 article outlines four aspects of heroism which brings to mind the stages of the hero's journey or quest described by Joseph Campbell, although Zimbardo later criticizes Campbell for putting heroes 'on a tall pedestal typically featuring male warriors' and maintains that 'the perpetuation of the myth of the "heroic elect" does society a disservice because it prevents the "average citizen" from considering their own heroic potential'.[26]

The first aspect is seen as 'some type of quest, which may range from the preservation of life to the preservation of an ideal'. Secondly 'heroism must have some form of actual or anticipated sacrifice or risk'. For Zimbardo this does not have to be an actual risk to life, as specified for those awarded the Carnegie medal, but may involve the risk of losing one's career or reputation as a result, for example of being a whistleblower. Thirdly 'the heroic act can either be passive or active' which would involve acts of passive resistance, and lastly 'heroism can be a sudden, one time act, or something that persists over a longer period of time'.[27] This aspect would cover those who take immediate action in an attempt to save the life of another or those who carry out a well thought out series of actions such as the rescuers of Jewish people during the Third Reich.

Zimbardo recognizes that some people are more likely than others to take part in the activities he describes, but unlike Kuszewski, who relates this difference to inherited personality traits, he believes that what is needed is the 'stimulation of heroic imagination'. This means 'the capacity to imagine facing physically or socially risky situations, to struggle with the hypothetical problems these situations generate, and to consider one's actions and the consequences'.[28] This in some way contradicts the work of Rand and Epstein who found that most acts of 'heroism' or extreme altruism are not carried out as a result of rational thought processes but are initiated by the fast, automatic, unconscious parts of the brain. It seems highly likely that having to imagine in advance all the consequences of one's actions when faced with a risky situation would inhibit most people from taking part in such actions rather than allowing them to transcend the possible costs involved.

Zimbardo and Franco include the possession of courage and fortitude as distinguishing features of the 'hero' but consider that 'inventors, athletes, actors, politicians and scientists', although serving as useful role models cannot be considered as 'heroes'. They consider that 'by diminishing the ideal of heroism . . . we dilute the important contribution of true heroes', but they fail to provide a definition of what is meant by a 'true hero'.[29] Many scientists for example have had to demonstrate considerable courage and fortitude in the face of opposition from colleagues and the public and sometimes even risked their lives in carrying out research which would benefit large numbers of people. People living under extreme hardship can demonstrate considerable fortitude if that means endurance, resilience and strength of mind, but most would not be considered as 'heroes'.

Zimbardo looks back to a time when 'words like bravery, fortitude, gallantry, and valor stirred our souls' and when 'children read of the exploits of great warriors and explorers and would set out to follow in those footsteps'.[30] This nostalgia for 'heroes' of the past with its militaristic undertones seems to suggest that children should be finding their inspiration in historical or even mythical figures who lived in times far removed from their own experience.

The difficulties that Zimbardo and his associates encounter when attempting to define the signifier 'hero' is hardly surprising, when, as has been shown, the word 'hero' is a mythical signifier to which people can attach their own meanings according to their own ideas, beliefs and purposes. In a later article, Franco, Blau and Zimbardo describe a detailed study they have carried out in an attempt to identify the characteristics required for an action to be considered as 'heroic' rather than merely altruistic, and they acknowledge the problems associated with the 'positive psychology view that heroism is always a virtuous, prosocial activity'.[31] In the study they identified certain figures who exemplified the 'broad conceptualization of heroism and who were deemed to be 'heroic' by the general public and the media', and then divided these into twelve 'heroic subtypes' depending on the situations that had driven their 'heroic' action. These included martial and civil heroism involving physical risk and ten variations of 'social heroism'. It is interesting that the latter included politicians and scientists, two categories that in their earlier article, Franco and Zimbardo maintained could not be considered as 'heroes'. They admit that the evaluation of a heroic act can depend on the experiences and personalities of those making the evaluation. For example someone entering a burning building to rescue a child may be viewed with admiration and awe by one person, but as 'foolhardy' by another person. Similarly someone acting as a whistle-blower may be acclaimed by many but regarded as a traitor by fellow workers. Another problem encountered in their study is the 'tension between the public's interpretation of the event and the private decision process of the hero', for although a particular action may be interpreted as heroic by witnesses, the supposed hero's actions may be the result of complex psychological and neurological processes rather than arising from a conscious decision to perform a prosocial 'heroic' act.

In carrying out the study, a total of 3,696 adults were recruited online and presented with hypothetical scenarios based on the identified 'heroic' categories. The martial and civil categories were broken down into five martial and five civil scenarios which were presented along with ten varieties of 'social heroism'. The participants were asked to identify each scenario as being either 'heroic', 'altruistic' or 'neither heroic, nor altruistic'.[32] Summarizing the results it was found that all the acts of martial heroism, such as a soldier dying so that others could escape, were rated as heroic by all the participants with each of the five acts receiving heroic status from more than sixty per cent. However, the act viewed as the most 'heroic' with 96 per cent of participants rating it as such, was civilian fire rescue, followed closely by a civilian wrestling a gun from a robber. In the 'social heroism' category only four out of the ten scenarios were rated as predominantly 'heroic' including politico-religious figures such as Martin Luther King, individuals who help others in need without necessarily incurring physical risk, and whistleblowers. Scientists, explorers and politicians were not considered as 'heroic' by the majority of participants, although religious figures and scientific discoverers were awarded high scores for altruism. The group which most people considered to be neither 'heroic' nor altruistic were martyrs, defined in this study as 'religious or political figures who knowingly put their lives in jeopardy in the service of a cause or an injustice'.

As part of their original hypotheses the study's authors speculated that acts of social heroism would be considered to be as heroic as those classified as military or civil, and in some cases even more heroic than those acts involving physical risk. In fact archetypal situations such as the civilian fire rescuer and the soldier laying down his life for a comrade received the highest ratings for 'heroism'; and as the authors suggest both of these acts contain certain 'cinematic elements that engender strong emotional responses', including rapid decision making and actions, and a strong element of suspense in view of the possible deaths of the victim and rescuer. The only acts in the social heroism category considered as heroic were those which involved fighting for a particular worthy cause or opposing bureaucratic injustice, both of which receive strong media and cinematic coverage.[33]

A further problem which arises in the interpretation of these results is the makeup of the sample which participated in the study. The authors themselves admit that 'the sample largely over-represents the views of White American young adult males' and presents a very 'American-centric' viewpoint. This is particularly relevant when seen in the context of recent American history in the years following the events of 9/11, and may help to explain the very negative response to the 'martyr' category. In each category the participants were given 'heroic' examples, most of which were taken from American history, such as Martin Luther King Jr. as a politico-religious figure and Abraham Lincoln as a political leader. Surprisingly the example for the martyr category was Socrates, for although he died because of his beliefs, choosing to take poison rather than renounce his criticism of current Athenian society and politics, his inclusion in the list of 'social heroes' raises many questions regarding the use of the word 'martyr' in the same context as 'hero'.

The original meaning of 'martyr' was 'witness' and came to be applied to a person who is persecuted or killed because of their religious or other beliefs. Christian martyrs were often referred to as 'heroes' and the two words were often inter-changeable. The idea of extreme altruism involving risk to one's life in the process of saving another, can only be relevant to martyrdom if acting to save the life of an individual is extended to cover sacrificing one's life for the sake of a cause or a belief or sometimes for a group or community. As has been previously discussed in the context of post-1982 Palestine, the signifier 'hero' can be applied to the self-sacrificing martyr or *shahid*, who is willing to die for the sake of their faith and their people. The use of the word 'martyr' in Franco, Blau and Zimbardo's study, as a category of social heroism would inevitably produce a negative response amongst the participants, as only ten years previously the terrorists who carried out the attacks of 9/11 killing nearly 3,000 innocent people had referred to themselves as martyrs.

Just as the signifier 'hero' is used by different groups of people to signify different concepts, so the word 'martyr' is used by different people at different times in history to signify people involved in widely different activities. A brief description of some of those referred to as martyrs will serve to illustrate this diversity. Socrates, as mentioned, chose to die rather than escape from Athens when he was charged by the state for corrupting the youth, and voluntarily drank poison from the cup offered to him. This may be seen as an act close to traditional martyrdom, that is death resulting from a refusal to renounce one's beliefs, but can in no way be considered as heroism as defined in the study. Martin Luther King Jr., who is included as an example in the politico-religious category, is considered by some to have been a martyr as he was assassinated because of his role in the Civil Rights Movement, but unlike Socrates and many Christian martyrs he did not choose to die. He was also awarded the highest score for heroism in the social heroism section of the study.

Some people have been seen as heroes, martyrs but also terrorists depending on the point of view of those making the judgment. Bobby Sands spent his childhood as part of a Catholic minority in North Belfast and suffered from sectarian discrimination and persecution by Ulster loyalists. In 1972 when he was eighteen he joined the Provisional IRA and was arrested on several occasions for the possession of guns, receiving a fourteen-year sentence in 1977. In 1981 he led a hunger strike for the reinstatement of Special Category status, the removal of which had resulted in the loss of certain rights for IRA prisoners, and he died from starvation in the Maze prison. It might be said that like Socrates he took his own life for the sake of his beliefs and he is seen by many in Ireland and throughout the world as a martyr but by many others as a terrorist who deserved to die. Another young man, living like Sands in the 1960s and 1970s, but in a very different part of the world, was Steve Biko who joined the anti-apartheid movement fighting against racial discrimination and white minority rule in South Africa. He formed his own Black Consciousness Movement which engaged in non-violent activities and he had a part in organizing the Soweto Uprising in 1976. In 1977 he was arrested for organizing protests and while in prison was tortured by state security officers, sustaining serious head injuries from which he died. Unlike Bobby Sands he did not choose to die although he must have realized that by organizing protests his life was at risk. Steve Biko is recognized as a martyr of the anti-apartheid movement and as a hero by most people throughout the world, but by the majority of white people living in South Africa at the time he would have been regarded as a terrorist.

Maybe the most typical example of a 'martyr' would be one of the many German people who openly resisted Nazi ideology during the Third Reich and as a result suffered persecution and death. Sophie Scholl, together with her brother Hans and student friends, formed a non-violent resistance group called the White Rose which printed and distributed anti-war leaflets. As a result of distributing leaflets in the University of Munich she was arrested, tried and executed by guillotine on 22 February 1943. She was a member of the Lutheran church and a devout Christian, meeting her death with equanimity and therefore conforming with the typical image of a Christian martyr.

Perhaps if the signifier 'martyr' is restricted to a single concept, that is a person who dies or is killed because of their beliefs, then its use is justified in that particular context, whereas the awarding of martyr status to the unintentional victims of violence seems somewhat perverse. The use of the word 'martyr' to describe those who in the process of killing themselves also kill many innocent people is totally inappropriate, for these so-called 'martyrs' are engaging in warfare against a perceived enemy and are not threatened with death if they refuse to relinquish their beliefs. It is hardly surprising that the participants in the study had such a negative response to a word which has recently acquired mainly negative associations.

Commenting on the results of their study, Franco, Blau and Zimbardo admit that heroism is not always a 'virtuous, prosocial' activity, and that there are many reasons why people engage in heroic acts. They do mention that other researchers have put forward the idea that heroic action may be 'a symptom of psychopathology or maladjustment', but Kuszewski's work on the characteristics shared by extreme altruists and sociopaths was published after the study described here. There is a brief mention of Pallone and Hennessey's work on 'heroic rescue fantasy' as a motivating factor in some heroic actions and there is a link here with

122 | THE MYTH OF THE MODERN HERO

certain psychoanalytical theories which will be discussed later, although their ideas should not be confused with Freud's 1910 work on 'rescue fantasy'.

Pallone and Hennessey identify certain features associated with 'heroic rescue fantasy' starting with the recognized observation that abnormal neuronal activity in certain brain areas can affect a person's ability to accurately assess the risks and benefits associated with a particular activity. This leads to impulsive rather than considered behavior and an underestimation of the risks associated with an activity. Information obtained from interviews with subjects indicated that a need for self-aggrandizement was often a factor and that this probably resulted from the subject's developmental experiences. They seemed to be particularly sensitive to situations where risk-taking activity would result in them being accepted as a role model and may actually create a situation involving risk to others and to themselves, on the successful completion of which they would be regarded as a hero and receive the desired praise and admiration. The behavior described is obviously highly abnormal but certain aspects such as impulsivity and the need for self-aggrandizement have been described by various researchers investigating so-called 'heroic' behavior.[34]

In addition to the work of Pallone and Hennessey and with a view to impartiality, Franco, Blau and Zimbardo refer to 'further negative views of heroism', although it is difficult to see how one can have a positive or negative view of a signifier which has been applied to many different concepts, most of which contain positive and negative aspects depending on the point of view of the group or individual using the signifier. One 'negative' view put forward in the discussion of the study is that so-called military heroism is often the result of certain physical and psychological factors associated with extreme combat conditions. The stress caused by these conditions – intense dependence on other group members, a complete dissociation from normal life and a deep hatred of and rage towards the enemy – may all encourage an individual to act impulsively and perform acts of so-called heroism without sufficient consideration of the possible results of their actions. The authors of the study describe how most nations use propaganda to 'instill hatred of their chosen enemies' amongst their citizens, and particularly amongst those members of the armed services sent to fight against these enemies. They use the phrase 'hostile imagination' to describe the way in which soldiers are made to think of the people in the land they are invading 'as objects, as unworthy, as less than human',[35] an attitude exemplified by Chris Kyle, who when fighting as a sniper in Iraq described the enemy as evil 'savages' who 'deserved to die'. Kyle as previously described was greeted as a great American 'hero'.

Franco and Zimbardo propose that 'hostile imagination' should be replaced by 'heroic imagination' which they describe as a 'mind-set, a collection of attitudes about helping others in need, beginning with caring for others in compassionate ways, but also moving toward a willingness to sacrifice or take risks on behalf of others or in defense of a moral cause'.[36] In their introduction to the study they suggest that 'heroism is viewed as distinct from other prosocial activities, such as compassion and altruism' and that 'the simple presence of risk accompanying prosocial behavior is not enough to define heroism'.[37] However, their definition of 'heroic imagination' does appear to be a definition that might be used by many to describe normal altruistic behavior, rather than the forms of extreme altruism generally referred to as 'heroism', and considered to be 'heroic' by the participants in their study.

The authors seem to imagine a world where people are compassionate, kind and helpful to one another, even if this is against their own interests, obviously an idealistic but very unrealistic view of human nature. In their 2011 paper Franco, Blau and Zimbardo admit that although 'the construct of heroic imagination' is central to their view of heroism, 'it remains largely theoretical and has not been adequately characterized to date'.[38] In 2010 an education director, Clint Wilkins, was appointed for the purpose of running pilot schemes for 'the Heroic Imagination Project' in two American high schools, and in 2012 he wrote an article for the American Psychological Association describing his experiences of running this project which 'provides lessons and tools to encourage "everyday heroism"'.[39] He writes of teaching

young people how to 'stand up, speak out and act courageously in challenging situations' and about 'the power
individuals and groups could have in bringing about positive
social change'. There is much discussion of the 'bystander
effect' in which people fail to react to a situation if they are
present as part of a group, the members of which also fail to
take action in a given situation. The 'everyday hero' is not
seeking to emulate the epic heroes of literature and myth, but
to perform 'extraordinary things in their communities'. This
does somewhat contradict the original views of the founder of
the project that the young should find inspiration in the stories
of mythical heroes like Achilles. School students were taught
how to handle negative peer pressure and confront bullying
and how to 'overcome prejudice by respecting individual
qualities'. All of this is of course very worthy, but contains little
to differentiate the project from established courses in social
psychology which aim to examine how individuals behave as
members of a group or a society. There are also similarities
with the Citizenship courses introduced as part of the National
Curriculum in the UK in 2002 and revised in 2014. These form
part of the 'spiritual, moral, social and cultural development'
aspects of the curriculum and aim to educate children to
become 'thoughtful, active citizens who engage with and
participate in public life'.[40] Zimbardo, in common with so
many others who choose to use the word 'hero', provides his
own definition, namely 'when the heroic imagination moti-
vates pro-social behavior it becomes heroic action. This kind
of behavior is labeled heroic'.[41] He does admit that 'there are
many interpretations of the word hero and the term heroic
action' but in his own writings he repeatedly suggests that to
qualify as 'heroic' an action must involve some kind of risk or
sacrifice, without which there is little to distinguish heroism
from altruism. Elizabeth Svoboda, a science writer who has
closely followed the work of Zimbardo, comments that
attempts to turn children into risk-taking heroes can cause
problems: 'If kids take the message of becoming heroes seriously, will heroism educators face blowback from parents
incensed that their children have been arrested for civil disobe-
dience – or have put their lives in danger trying to rescue a

pedestrian from the path of a speeding train?'[42] Zimbardo's colleague, Zeno Franco, questions the idea of a heroic education program, pointing out that if children are asked 'to engage around the idea of heroism but diminish the idea down to where it's safe, it loses its fundamental power'.[43] Zimbardo considers that children can be warned not to take unnecessary risks but surely this negates the presumption that heroism, as defined by most people, is about taking risks. His view, as described by Svoboda, that heroism is 'fundamentally about showing moral courage, and most "everyday hero" acts, like standing up to bullies, don't have to involve putting yourself in dire danger',[44] is very much in line with ideas incorporated into social education and citizenship programs, but without any mention of heroism.

In 2007 a colleague of Zimbardo at Stanford University, the neurosurgeon, Jim Doty, was responsible for setting up the Center for Compassion and Altruism Research and Education (CCARE) within the School of Medicine at Stanford, an enterprise made possible by a personal donation of 150,000 dollars from the Dalai Lama. The setting up of such a center within a scientific institution and the source of its finance may have seemed incongruous to some people, but studies such as those of Rand and Epstein and Andrea Kuszeweski have been directed towards establishing the biological processes associated with altruistic behavior. CCARE organized a 'Science of Compassion' conference in 2012 in Telluride, Colorado during which various researchers presented evidence obtained from brain imaging studies in which certain brain areas showed increased activity when subjects expressed compassionate feelings. This is obviously important for those neuroscientists working to establish the relationship between brain activity and emotional states but does little to explain the complex factors motivating extreme altruism and so-called heroism. Svoboda, who attended the conference, describes the casual and friendly approach of the attendees and presenters who eagerly collect brochures advertising programs in Buddhist studies, 'eat gluten-free cookies, or purchase CCARE T-shirts that say GOT COMPASSION'. The link between CCARE, Doty and the Dalai Lama has been criticized by some people who question whether CCARE can conduct valid scientific research when, according to Svoboda, 'some of its researchers subscribe, in whole or in part, to Buddhist principles – and when its most famous private donor is the most prominent Buddhist leader on the planet'.[45] An important question is whether these Buddhist principles will affect the way studies are designed and interpreted, in other words can they be truly objective. Philip Zimbardo's link with CCARE is perhaps somewhat unfortunate as his study aiming to differentiate between heroic action and altruism is predominantly based on objective and analytical research. Svoboda notes that at one CCARE conference Zimbardo asked the Dalai Lama, 'Is compassion enough in a world filled with evil? How do we go beyond compassion, which is the highest personal virtue, to heroism, which is the highest civic virtue?'[46] Zimbardo recognizes that the possession of compassion and altruism are not sufficient to qualify someone as a 'hero' under his definition of the word, but the word 'evil' has religious connotations, conjuring up a picture of a supernatural force which must be defeated by the good and virtuous. Zimbardo himself has admitted that heroism is not always a virtuous activity and yet he writes of heroic action as being 'the antidote to evil', and the idea of some that the 'fundamental contribution of heroes is "saving the soul of a nation."' When he says that one of the functions of the 'Heroic Imagination Project' is to fortify people against the 'allure of the dark side', his use of a term associated with the *Star Wars* films is perhaps an allusion to this battle between good and evil, an association made much of by Joseph Campbell who sees the films of George Lucas as an interpretation of the heroic myth.[47]

A critical examination of the work of Zimbardo and Doty and their associates is important because much of the research now referred to as 'Heroism Science' is related in some way to the 'Heroic Imagination Project' or the Centre for Compassion and Altruism Research and Education. Although both of these projects carry out important work, making people aware of the need for caring for others in society and encouraging children to make a stand against injustice, neither of them seem to have very much to do with heroism as defined by most members of society, including those who took part in Franco, Blau and Zimbardo's study on the difference between heroic action and altruism. In the popular imagination the 'hero' is still someone who carries out an act of extreme bravery, usually involving some risk to themselves, in other words the archetypal hero of myth and legend, but if the word 'hero' is, as I have proposed, a mythical signifier, it can be made to mean anything the user wishes it to mean. The emergence in the last ten years of the cross-disciplinary field of 'Heroism Science' has produced many and varied interpretations of the signifier 'hero', which might suggest that the word itself has become redundant and should be replaced by words which more accurately represent the activities described. In the introduction to the 'Heroism Science Conference 2016' held at Murdoch University in Perth, acknowledgement is given to Franco and Zimbardo's paper 'The Banality of Heroism' for 'catapulting heroism into the realm of scientific enquiry'.[48] If 'science' is taken to mean a 'body of knowledge on any subject' then the use of the word here is valid, but if, as generally interpreted, it means the study of 'the physical and natural world through observation and experiment', then most of the papers presented at the conference would not be considered to be scientific. The six categories included in the conference were historical perspectives, cultural perspectives, heroism in popular culture and fiction, contemporary psychological perspectives, heroism in professional contexts and career identity, and heroism in educational contexts. There was no category for scientific perspectives such as 'the neurophysiology and evolutionary origins of heroism' as had been suggested in the initial publicity for the conference. No doubt the conference was useful and informative but the question has to be asked as to why a need is felt for the introduction of a new discipline 'Heroism Science' when most of the topics discussed are covered by specialists in other disciplines using appropriate nomenclature relevant to these disciplines.

It seems that there is considerable difference of opinion amongst researchers in this field as to the boundaries which exist between the ideas of altruism, extreme altruism and heroism, and these differences appear to be even more divergent when attempts are made to attach a meaning to the idea of 'altruism'. Fogelman, in discussing the motives of those who helped the Jews in Nazi-occupied Europe, writes of the 'ego gratification and self-satisfaction' many of them gained from their activities and psychoanalysts argue that unconscious, self-gratification lies behind most acts of perceived altruism. Anna Freud, in *The Ego and the Mechanisms of Defense*, put forward the idea that pure altruistic motivation does not exist, and expanded on her father's belief that altruism was one of the many defense mechanisms utilized to protect the ego and enable a person to cope with anxiety.[49] She used the term 'altruistic surrender' to describe the behavior she observed in a 'group of inhibited individuals who were neurotically driven to do good for others'.[50] Beth Seelig and Lisa Rosof in their paper 'Normal and Pathological Altruism' seek to re-examine this view of altruism and propose five distinct categories of altruism. Protoaltruism is the instinctive behavior seen in all animals, including humans, which is particularly evident in the care and protection of the young and is obviously essential to survival. The psychologist Stephanie Preston has studied the behavior of mother rats who repeatedly retrieve young rats who wander off regardless of whether they are their own offspring or not. Using brain imaging techniques she has found that there is increased activity in the amygdala region of the rat's brain during this retrieval activity, mirroring exactly the activity observed in this part of the brain in human subjects when engaging in altruistic behavior.[51] Generative altruism refers to the 'ability to experience conflict-free pleasure in fostering the success and/or pleasure of another',[52] and is based on the possession of empathy, that is sharing in the feelings of another person, without engaging in altruistic actions. The third type of altruism is referred to as 'conflicted altruism', the features of which come close to Anna Freud's idea of 'altruistic surrender'. Here the performing of altruistic acts, like those carried out by the rescuers of Jews, provides considerable pleasure and satisfaction for those carrying out the acts, in other words they are rewarded for their actions. In contrast, pseudoaltruism 'involves efforts to defend against profound aggression, envy, and a superego-driven need to suffer and be a victim', and no pleasure is obtained from the carrying out of the altruistic act. These 'self-denying martyrs' unconsciously use their self-sacrificing acts to protect their egos against their aggressive drives. Seelig and Rosof describe the case of a young woman who 'felt that it was very important to do good for others She took great pride in the self-sacrifice and suffering involved in spending long hours doing things she hated as a service to other people'.[53] The fifth category of altruism defined is psychotic altruism and is 'demonstrated by individuals whose delusions drive them to damage or sacrifice themselves for the welfare of others'.[54] Although not usually considered as psychotic some acts of extreme altruism or 'heroism', particularly martyrdom may be placed in this category.

The general view adopted by psychoanalysts is that all altruistic behavior occurs as a result of conflict, and due to the influence of Anna Freud 'the term altruism has often been used as an abbreviation for altruistic surrender, and thus has been seen as pathological'.[55] Seelig and Rosof, by distinguishing between different forms of altruism, attempt to show that an individual who experiences pleasure from helping others is not necessarily compensating for an inability to fulfill their own desires. They acknowledge that protoaltruism has a biological basis as a survival mechanism, and Smirnov et al., as previously discussed, have suggested a possible mechanism whereby extreme altruism might have evolved in hunter-gatherer societies. Generative altruism, which involves the expression of empathy, seems to coincide with the normal idea of altruism as the display of compassion, but according to Zimbardo and others altruism also involves the performing of acts to assist others, bringing this type of behavior into Seelig and Rostof's category of 'conflicted altruism' and 'altruistic surrender'. The possibility that every time we perform an altruistic or compassionate act to help others we are unconsciously seeking to gratify our own egos might not be acceptable to the majority, but evidence such as that provided by Fogelman resulting from her conversations with rescuers of Jews, does indicate that the possibility exists.

Franco, Blau and Zimbardo, in discussing the results of their study on the difference between altruism and heroism, admit that a supposed heroic action may result from complex psychological and neurological processes taking place in the brain of the apparent 'hero', and Seelig and Rostof identify some of these processes in their last two categories of altruism. For the pseudoaltruist no pleasure is derived from their altruistic act which is carried out to defend against 'libidinal and aggressive drives.' The authors consider that this category includes 'many joyless and self-denying martyrs with severe masochistic and narcissistic pathology'.[56] This definition may apply to certain religious martyrs but does not seem appropriate for the so-called martyrs I have discussed in this chapter.

Psychoanalysts make a distinction between the seemingly positive act of normal altruism, in which a person receives conflict-free pleasure from helping others, and the pathological type of altruism in which a person has a need to sacrifice themselves for the benefit of others. In psychoanalytical terms this sacrifice does not usually involve injury or death but the sacrifice of an individual's own needs and drives in the defense of their ego. Pallone and Hennessy's model for the heroic rescue fantasy involving a need for self-aggrandizement and the creation of opportunities to enact a heroic rescue which elicits praise and admiration, does not conform with the psychoanalytical theory described here and is based on psychological theories related to an individual's psychosocial development.

The psychoanalytical view of altruism as an ego defense mechanism has some commonality with Nietzsche's idea that no action is entirely selfless or 'non-egoistic', and Freud himself said that Nietzsche's 'premonitions and insights often agree in the most amazing manner with the laborious results of psychoanalysis'.[57] Nietzsche rejected the values and morality of the bourgeois Christian society in which he lived and believed that there was another set of values, not imposed by society but arising from human nature and the natural demands of the body. In *The Genealogy of Morals* he describes the values of the Judeo-Christian tradition as supporting the view that 'the wretched are alone the good; the poor, the weak, the lowly, are alone the good; the suffering, the needy, the sick, . . . are the only ones who are blessed . . . but you men of power, you are to all eternity the evil, the horrible, the covetous, the insatiate, the godless, . . . the cursed, the damned!'[58] For Nietzsche this 'slave' morality has become accepted as the norm in society for two millennia and he proposes a new 'master' morality which is noble, powerful and self-secure, reflecting human excellence. In this new morality the highest good anyone can attain is in relation to their own, individual state of being rather than in concern for others. He saw that the Greek philosophers such as Plato and Aristotle did not exhibit sympathy for others but fought for their own egos. In *The Dawn*, he says, 'The greatest marvels of antiquity, such as Epictetus, knew nothing of the glorification, now so common, of the spirit of sacrifice, of living for others: after the fashion of morality now prevailing we should really call them immoral; for they fought with all their strength for their own ego and against all sympathy for others'.[59] In other words self-perfection and self-mastery are part of the 'Will to Power' and the ideal goal of the *Übermensch*.

Walter Kaufmann in discussing Nietzsche's 'repudiation of altruism' says: 'According to Nietzsche, pity is bad both for those who feel it and for those who are being pitied. It is bad for the pitied because it does not help them toward happiness and perfection and well-being . . . A religion that preaches pity assumes that suffering is bad . . . self-perfection, however is possible only through suffering, and the ultimate happiness of the man who has overcome himself does not exclude suffering'.[60] Nietzsche's use of the word pity implies compassion but also 'active' altruism, or using the classification system of Seelig and Rosof, 'conflicted altruism'. He suggests that, in performing an altruistic act we are depending on the person we show pity towards to defend our egos, rather than building our own egos or 'state of being', in other words 'thinking of One's Self'. In *The Dawn* he poses the question, 'Let us seriously consider why we should jump into the water to rescue someone who has just fallen in before our eyes, although we may have no particular sympathy for him'.[61] The answer expected is 'out of pity', but Nietzsche says that 'in our pity . . . we no longer think consciously of ourselves, but quite unconsciously, exactly as when slipping we unconsciously make the best counter-motions possible in order to recover our balance'.[62] He recalls an incident when, while walking along the street, a man collapsed and fell down in front of him and describes how he 'set the man on his feet again and waited until he recovered his speech. During this time no muscle of my face moved, and I experienced no sensation of fear or pity . . . and calmly proceeded on my way'.[63] This contrasted with the behavior of the surrounding crowd who cried out in horror. He imagines what would have happened if he had been told the day before that such an incident would occur and faces the possibility that he would have 'suffered all kinds of agonies . . . lying awake all night, and at the decisive moment should also perhaps have fallen down like the man instead of helping him; for in the meantime all the imaginable cravings within me would have had leisure to conceive and to comment upon this incident'.[64] Nietzsche seems to be comparing here the automatic, intuitive, unemotional response to a situation, as described by Rand and Epstein, and the deliberative, conscious response.

Nietzsche appears to be looking forward to Freud's ego defense mechanisms and Anna Freud's theory of 'altruistic surrender', when he says 'it is thus only this personal feeling of misery that we get rid of by acts of compassion' and 'as it is certain that we wish to free ourselves from suffering thereby, it is also certain that by the same action we yield to an impulse of pleasure' and 'the thought of the praise and gratitude which we would gain if we did help'.[65] Nietzsche considered that the 'cult of altruism' and the 'preaching of altruistic morality in the service of individual egoism' is 'one of the most common lies of the nineteenth century',[66] and is the result of being subjected to hundreds of years of Christian or 'slave' morality. If a person performs an act of extreme altruism which involves putting their own life at risk in order to save the life of another person, that person would generally be considered to be a 'hero'. However, in risking their own life the rescuer is unwittingly accepting that the other person's life is worth more than their own. According to Seelig and Rosof's categories of altruism, such extreme altruistic acts are defined as psychotic rather than 'heroic', or as Nietzsche puts it, 'danger and aberration lies in disinterested and selfless actions'.[67]

FIVE

Not Heroes,
Just Human Beings

The hero myth is one of the most potent creations of the human mind, firing people's imaginations and prompting the belief that, even in modern times, there are certain individuals who act in ways which qualify them to receive the accolade of 'hero', people who are braver and more courageous than most of us could ever be and who deserve our admiration and respect. It is generally accepted that for an act to be considered as 'heroic' it must be witnessed and recognized as such, in other words it is always the onlooker of the deed who awards the accolade of 'hero'. Two problems arise from this, the first being that the witness cannot have a full knowledge of the motives or internal state of mind of the 'hero', and secondly that the unrecognized person performing a courageous act or living a life of courage and endurance cannot be regarded as 'heroic'. Franco, Blau and Zimbardo in their study of heroism admit that there is a conflict between the public interpretation of an act and the private decision making, whether conscious or unconscious, of the person performing the act. They also acknowledge the existence of 'unsung heroes' who perform what might be recognized as heroic deeds if witnesses had been present. This is particularly relevant in the case of military actions in which there may be no survivors or at least no witnesses to the 'heroic' act.

During the war in Afghanistan, a young British soldier in the Royal Gurkha Rifles, Dip Prasad Pun, was alone on sentry duty at a checkpoint guarding the unit's compound, when he saw two Taliban fighters laying IEDs at the compound's gate. The checkpoint was soon surrounded but Dip Prasad Pun remained on the roof and was attacked continuously with rocket-propelled grenades and AK47s. He returned fire with his machine gun, hand grenades and a Claymore mine, even attacking one insurgent with the metal tripod of his machine gun. Over the course of just 15 minutes he had defeated about fifteen insurgents and saved the lives of three fellow soldiers who were at the checkpoint, preventing the position from being overrun. He had reported the situation to his commanding officer by radio, who arrived just in time to see the surviving insurgents fleeing from the scene. Sergeant Pun said afterwards that he felt certain that he was going to die and so he tried to kill as many as he could, adding that as soon as he started firing any feeling of fear went away. His action was obviously very courageous but if his situation and background are considered it becomes clear that no other action would have been possible. Like all Gurkha soldiers, Pun came from a tight-knit rural community in Nepal where qualities of endurance and ingenuity are essential for survival. The selection procedure is rigorous and for a family member to be selected is a source of great pride and of course respect from the whole community. Pun's father and grandfather were also Gurkhas, and the possibility of letting his community, his family and his fellow soldiers down would have been unthinkable. The motto of the Royal Gurkha Rifles is "Better to die than be a coward", and the alternative action in this situation of leaving his position and allowing the insurgents to take over the compound was something that could not be contemplated. It might be concluded that Pun did not consciously choose to perform a heroic act but that this was the sort of automatic, intuitive process observed by Rand and Epstein in their study of Carnegie medal recipients. Pun's act was witnessed and he was awarded the Conspicuous Gallantry Cross for an act of bravery.[1]

On the first day of the Somme offensive during World War One, Private Henry Russell of the London Rifle Brigade advanced towards enemy lines and as colleagues dropped down around him he continued to go forward, suddenly becoming aware that 'there were few of us in this first line of attack capable of going on'. Together with an officer,

Lieutenant Wallace, he dived into a shallow hole in the ground and realized that they were completely surrounded by German soldiers. The officer stood up and was immediately shot down, 'riddled with bullets'. Russell also stood up in the vain hope that he might be able to 'pick off' some Germans, but was immediately hit by two bullets, 'one from behind and one from in front'. Reflecting on his actions later he says 'I had thought that a man who could stand up and knowingly face practically certain death in these circumstances must be very brave. I found out that bravery hardly came into it. Once the decision was made to stand up I had no further fear. I was not bothered at all even though I believed that I would be dead within seconds . . . I am now convinced that when it comes to the last crunch nobody has any fear at all; it is not a question of bravery. In some extraordinary manner, the chemistry of the body anesthetizes it in such a way that, even when fully conscious, fear does not enter into the matter'.[2] Russell's comments correspond with those of Pun who admitted feeling no fear when he started firing at the enemy. The idea that the body chemistry prepares the body for action and temporarily at least inhibits feelings of fear is well known, and is similar to the *thumos* described by Homer in relation to the warrior Achilles. Russell, despite his severe wounds managed to crawl back towards the British lines under heavy shellfire, stopping on the way to help a wounded soldier lying in a shell hole. The soldier was killed when the shell hole was hit by a particularly heavy barrage of shellfire and Russell received further serious injuries from this attack. He managed to drag himself back to the British lines but of course there were no witnesses to his actions. Richard Van Emdon notes that by the end of the war 'while large numbers of men had been recognized for bravery, clearly the vast majority had received nothing; although they might have been equally courageous, their actions went unnoticed'. Some soldiers commented that Military Medals (MM), a gallantry award for NCOs and other ranks, 'were sent up with the rations, to be distributed as largesse by an officer', and that 'there was no clear policy for its award'. This resulted in the award of medals to those who had served well behind the lines and may 'never have seen a shell burst or heard enemy rifle fire'.[3] Honors for acts of bravery in battle have been awarded since the time of the ancient Greeks and for warriors like Achilles the receiving of honors and the achievement of glory provided the motivation for all military action. As Angela Hobbs points out however, Achilles was well aware of the 'link between heroic death and glory', and although he realizes 'that if he succeeds in killing Hector . . . then his own death is imminent', he still vows to 'win excellent glory'. Hobbs comments on Achilles' awareness that 'the obtaining of glory will usually require risking, or even seeking, the very death that he abhors'.[4] The soldiers of World War One had no interest in winning glory and did not see themselves as 'heroes', they simply wished to survive the situations into which they had been placed without being given any prior warning of the horrors they were to experience. The awarding of medals under these conditions seems somewhat super-fluous when the majority of combatants on the front line were performing acts of extreme bravery on a daily basis, with no opportunity for individual recognition.

The conflict between the public interpretation of an act and the inner mental processes of the person performing the act is satirized by Winston Groom in his 1986 'comic' novel *Forrest Gump*, in which he presents a fictional but very realistic portrayal of the conditions experienced by American soldiers in the Vietnam War, and which has much to say about the public perception of the 'hero'.[5] Gump makes his way through life, never being quite aware of what is going on around him. He says that he has an IQ of 'near 70' and likes to think of himself as a *'halfwit'*, but his big advantage is his height of six foot six, his weight and strength, and his ability to run very fast. This ability results in him becoming the 'hero' of the local football team for, despite the fact that he cannot understand the rules of the game, he can run very fast with the ball when prompted to do so. He is drafted into the army and after a year of being 'trained like robots' he learns that he is being sent off to somewhere 10,000 miles away, to a place called Vietnam. At first he sees this as a great adventure but soon faces the reality of an attack and the horror of seeing dead and mangled bodies. Because of his strength and size he is made to carry most of the equipment and supplies as they move through the jungle and willingly complies with all demands. He has no understanding of who is fighting who or why they are fighting, and when he sees a large group of enemy soldiers approaching thinks to himself that the best thing they can do is to try to make friends with them, obviously not an option. During a particularly bad attack with many of his Company killed, he sees that one man is still breathing, and so he picks him up and throws him over his shoulder and starts running with him through the brush towards his Company, with enemy bullets whizzing all around him. He finds himself in an area where he is surrounded by the enemy and starts to run at full speed 'bellowin an hollerin loud as I can an runnin for dear life'. He reaches his Company and discovers that the enemy soldiers were so frightened by the noise he was making that they ran away. He is congratulated by the Company commander but when asked how he managed to do it he cannot answer, his strength and his speed being part of his nature. A few weeks later, when again surrounded by the enemy, Gump realizes that his friend Bubba is missing, and learning that he has been wounded he runs out into the rice paddy to rescue him. On the way he finds another badly wounded soldier and picks him up and runs back with him, 'bullets an stuff flyin all over', thinking to himself 'it is something I simply cannot understand – why in hell is we doin all this, anyway? Playin football is one thing. But this, I do not know why.' He runs back to find Bubba and carries him back to comparative safety, but it is too late and Bubba dies from his wounds. In the ensuing fighting Gump himself is wounded and is airlifted out to hospital. While recovering in hospital he receives visitors from Field Force Headquarters who tell him that he has been awarded the Congressional Medal of honor for extreme heroism and is to be flown back to the USA to be decorated by the President. The colonel accompanying him on the flight back tells him what a 'great hero' he is going to be when they get back to the United States and how a big crowd will be waiting to greet him. There is indeed a big crowd but not the sort the colonel expected. About two thousand anti-war protestors, waving banners and shouting 'nasty things', even throwing tomatoes at them, rushed towards them as they came off the plane, and Gump at least was able to run fast to the terminal to escape them. It reminds him of how he ran across the paddy field when his friend Bubba was killed and he feels just as frightened as he did then. In Washington they go to the White House where he is greeted as a 'hero' by the 'Army people', and has his medal pinned on his chest by the President. His next duty is to take part in a recruitment tour to get people to enlist in the army, but Gump has difficulty with remembering the speech he is meant to deliver and is heckled by people in the crowd. Suddenly someone shouts out to him, 'What do you think of the war?', and without pausing for thought he replies, using somewhat strong language, that he thinks it is hateful, pointless and rubbish. Gump's career as a war hero is obviously over at this point but Winston Groom's cynical take on the making of a 'hero' in the Vietnam War is an excellent comment on the mythical nature of the 'hero' and the motives behind a seemingly heroic act. Gump is a kind, compassionate person, always ready to see good in others, in other words an altruist, but his main outstanding qualities which enable him to perform 'heroic' deeds are his great strength and his ability to run very fast. Gump does not understand why he is in Vietnam, what he is fighting for, or who he is fighting against, thinking at one point that 'maybe it is the Dutch – or even the Norwegians – who knows?' He does however perform two courageous acts which would be considered by most people to be heroic and which are recognized as such by his commanding officers. When he picks up the wounded soldier and runs with him at full speed it is almost as if he is taking part in a football game, not quite understanding the rules but knowing that he has to run as fast as he can. Just as he shows loyalty to the members of his football team he has no hesitation in rushing to help his fellow soldiers. He does not, however, feel that he is fighting for his country, or for any particular cause and feels that the best course of action would be to make friends with the enemy. His rapid, automatic actions to rescue his friends are the same as those recognized by Rand and Epstein in their study of Carnegie Medal recipients, and he intuitively knows that he has the strength and physical ability to perform the rescues. However, for those who award him the medal he is the true military, patriotic hero, fighting to defeat the enemies of his country. For the crowd of protestors demonstrating at the airport he is no hero, for he has been taking part in what they see as a pointless war, engaged in by their country because of their fear of the spread of communism, a war which resulted in the deaths of thousands of American soldiers. Although in risking his life to rescue a fellow soldier, he might seem to fulfill the criteria to be recognized as a military hero, Gump's behavior in rescuing a friend in need seems to fit more easily into Seelig and Rosof's category of protoaltruism, an instinctive behavior which does not reward the rescuer with any feeling of pleasure.

Franco, Blau and Zimbardo acknowledge the existence of other problems when considering whether a person should be awarded the accolade of 'hero', and refers to these as "Heroization" and 'Retrospective Bias'. Judgements as to the worthiness of the prospective 'hero' may be based, not just on the nature of the 'heroic' act, but on the personality and moral character of the person carrying out the act. Particularly in the case of social heroism, factors such as social standing, leadership ability, communication skills and even 'whether or not the person "looks the part"', may all play a part in determining the award of heroic status.[6] O.E. Klapp, in a 1954 paper looking at the public perception of heroes, says,

> Rationality, therefore should not be stressed as a factor in recognition of heroes . . . most of such typing probably occurs by a spontaneous popular definition in which there is little reflective thought . . . Among the important non-rational processes which help to form heroes and antiheroes are gossip, rumor, propaganda, journalism . . . , social crisis mentality, and the accidents of publicity and opportunity which have helped make some men famous and obscured others equally deserving of credit.[7]

Written long before the advent of mass social media, this view seems somewhat prophetic. The problem of 'retrospective bias' is important in cases of so-called social heroism, some time often having to pass before the full impact of a person's actions come to be fully understood, and even then there may be political or religious controversy over whether a person should be considered a 'hero'. In fact, as Zimbardo points out, it might be the death of the supposed 'hero' that provides the emotional stimulus for proclaiming their heroic status.

An important source of evidence for the existence of both 'heroization' and 'retrospective bias', is found within the history of the American Civil Rights Movement. In Franco, Blau and Zimbardo's study, the highest score for heroism in the social heroism category was given to Martin Luther King Jr., his score coming just behind those of the civilian fire rescuer and the soldier who dies so that others can escape. No one can deny the enormous contribution made by King to the Civil Rights Movement in the 1950s and 1960s, but there are many others who made an equal if not greater contribution and some, who by risking their lives for the cause in which they believed surely deserve equal recognition. Most of these people would not see themselves as 'heroes', just human beings fighting for the right to be recognized as such. Many of those working in the Civil Rights Movement believed that emphasis should be placed on groups of people working together to produce plans of action, rather than acting on instructions received from the leaders of the large Civil Rights organizations, in other words 'group-centered leadership' rather than a 'leader-centered group'. This type of organization would of course work against the emergence of charismatic leaders who would be praised for achievements made and serve as figureheads for the movement, eventually being regarded as the true 'heroes' in the struggle for equality.

One person responsible more than any other for the development and success of the mass civil movement was Ella Baker who, in the words of J. Todd Moye, 'wielded tremendous influence over a generation of social activists, even if she was invisible and unknown to the majority of Americans then and remains so now'. Baker's theory was that 'strong people don't need strong leaders', and she shunned personal publicity.[8] The historian Charles Payne writes that she had 'faith that ordinary people who learn to believe in themselves are capable of extraordinary acts, or better, of acts that seem extraordinary to us precisely because we have such an impoverished sense of the capabilities of ordinary people'.[9] These people are seldom identified as 'heroes' because they don't conform with the public's expectations of what a 'hero' should be, that is an individual person performing a 'heroic' deed , however that may be defined.

Born in 1903, Baker, the granddaughter of slaves, was brought up in rural North Carolina where her family had worked hard to acquire farming land and were part of what might be considered to be a middle-class black community. The Church was very important in this community and women played a significant role in church affairs, 'conducting their own meetings, managing their finances, and making policy decisions'. This early experience of group and particularly female group action had considerable influence on Baker in her later work with civil rights groups, and made her particularly wary of 'hierarchical and male dominated' institutions'.[10] Baker attended the renowned black, Shaw University in North Carolina, where she took part in debates, edited the student newspaper and challenged some of the strict rules resulting from the university's affiliation with the Baptist church. Lack of funds prevented her from attending graduate school in Chicago, instead she went to live in New York which proved to be an important step in determining the course of her future career. She immersed herself in the thriving and exciting cultural and social life of Harlem, debating with and becoming influenced by black socialists and reading Marx for the first time in the New York Public Library. After the stock market crash of 1929 she began work as a freelance journalist, writing articles on economic issues for various black newspapers and journals. It is worth noting that in the same year Martin Luther King Jr. was born in Atlanta, Georgia, and his and Baker's paths were to cross nearly thirty years later when King formed the Southern Christian Leadership Conference (SCLC), and Baker realized that their ideas on the organization of mass protest were very different. The publisher George Schuyler introduced Baker to the Young Negroes' Cooperative League (YNCL) and in 1931 she was appointed national director, responsible for organizing a network of local cooperative groups. This was Baker's first experience of group-centered action in which she acted as facilitator and advisor, but it was the young group members, both men and women, who made the important decisions related to the particular problems in their local area. Unfortunately the dire economic problems of the 1930s led to a decrease in the numbers of contributing members and only a small number of groups managed to survive. The YNCL, however, gave many young black people the opportunity to organize themselves into effective groups and for Baker it provided valuable experience for her future roles in the Civil Rights Movement. For the next few years Baker worked on various educational and community projects in New York including the Workers Education Project, part of President Roosevelt's New Deal, and this brought her into contact with teachers who 'openly espoused socialist ideas' or who were active members of the Communist Party.[11] She believed that education would help to empower disadvantaged black people enabling them to work together to construct their own plans of action. In 1941 Baker applied for a position in the national office of the National Association for the Advancement of Colored People (NAACP), and was appointed as assistant field secretary. To quote Moye 'this was the job that would change Baker's life. She went to work full time as an advocate for the civil rights of African Americans' and according to historian Patricia Sullivan she 'cultivated the militancy and expectations unleashed by the war, helping to shape the fuller contours of a southern movement'.[12]

In the early 1940s, when Baker was beginning her work for the NAACP, a young, black teenager, whose father was a minister in the Baptist church, was growing up in Atlanta, Georgia and beginning to experience the iniquities of segregation and the Jim Crow laws of the South. This teenager was Martin Luther King who, in his autobiography, recalls an incident when he travelled by bus with his teacher to a town some distance away to take part in an 'oratorical contest'. Even at this young age King's oratorical skills were evident and he won the contest speaking on 'The Negro and the Constitution'. On the way back some white passengers boarded the bus and the white driver ordered them to get up and give the whites their seats. King wanted to stay in his seat but his teacher was unwilling to break the law and they stood for the ninety miles to Atlanta. He says 'that night will never leave my memory. It was the angriest I have ever been in my life'.[13]

The NAACP had been founded in 1909 and was the main national organization working for civil rights. Martin Luther King's father was actually the president of the local NAACP branch in Atlanta. The emphasis of the organization was to bring cases of racial injustice to the courts and consequently to abolish Jim Crow state laws through the rulings of the federal courts. Baker could see that this policy could only work if individual states agreed to obey the rulings but this was not the case, as demonstrated by the continued enforcement of segregation on buses in Southern states. The NAACP was certainly a leader centered rather than a group centered organization with instructions passing down to local groups from the national office in New York, and officers of local branches mainly being prominent figures in the local community such as Martin Luther King Sr. Baker's work for the NAACP involved travelling widely through the South, publicizing the work of the organization, and increasing group membership, with the aim of producing a truly mass movement. She addressed numerous meetings and spoke to student and church groups, emphasizing the importance of local action to solve local problems. She also experienced the segregation laws first hand, when she was forcibly removed by police from her seat in a dining car, when she was travelling by train between Miami and New York. Her criticism of top down leadership in the NAACP extended to a criticism of many African American ministers in the Baptist Church who considered that the congregations should follow their lead rather than formulating their own ideas for action. In 1943 Baker was appointed as National Director of Branches for the NAACP and set about devising policies which would give members of local branches more say in developing programs and increasing member numbers. Charles Payne notes how 'she urged the organization to recruit more low-income members by, for example, sending organizers into pool rooms and taverns'.[14] She organized a series of regional leadership conferences and training sessions on issues such as school desegregation and voting rights, one of these conferences in Atlanta being attended by the secretary of the Montgomery, Alabama branch, Rosa Parks. Parks, who was accustomed to working almost exclusively with chauvinistic men, was very impressed with Baker, describing her as being 'smart and funny and strong' and giving her 'a new sense of purpose'.[15] The two women became firm friends and with Baker's encouragement Parks began to play a bigger role in her local NAACP branch, culminating nine years later in the Montgomery bus protest.

Baker, however, was becoming increasingly dissatisfied with her role in the NAACP, feeling that her views on policy were disregarded by the other, all male leaders of the organization in New York, and in 1946 she resigned from her role as national director of branches. Moye points out that after Baker departed 'the nation's most important civil rights organization never took advantage of its most valuable resource, its people, to foment a mass movement'.[16] The experience Baker had gained in working with NAACP branches in the South was not wasted, for the large number of contacts she had made and the methods of working she had encouraged were to be of considerable use in her work with new organizations which were to spring up in the 1950s and 1960s. In 1954 Baker joined with two New York activists, Stanley Levison and Bayard Rustin, to form the 'In Friendship' organization which raised money to assist those in Southern states who had suffered violence and persecution from white groups set up to maintain racial segregation in schools despite a US Supreme Court decision which made segregation illegal.

Baker was not at first directly involved with the Montgomery bus boycott but it was in Montgomery, when the boycott had successfully brought an end to segregation on the transport system, that she met Martin Luther King Jr. for the first time. Having completed his studies for his doctorate at Boston University in 1954, King was appointed as minister of Dexter Avenue Baptist church in Montgomery and within a few months found himself involved in the largest mass resist-

146 | THE MYTH OF THE MODERN HERO

ance movement against Southern segregation laws that had so far taken place. Although profoundly aware of the inequities of the present system in the South, King had not become involved in any action group or Civil Rights organization, but as part of his studies had read widely and absorbed the ideas of many who advocated nonviolent resistance. He joined the Montgomery branch of the NAACP and it was on December 1st, 1955 that Rosa Parks, the secretary of the branch, was arrested for refusing to give up her seat to a white passenger who had just boarded the bus. In his autobiography King praises Rosa Parks for her 'dignified manner' and 'radiant personality' and describes her as being 'a victim of both the forces of history and the forces of destiny'.[17] He fails to mention that Parks was a prominent member of the NAACP, attending regional meetings and speaking at conferences, and shortly before the boycott had attended a two-week workshop at the Highlander Folk School in Tennessee where desegregation activities had been discussed. Moye observes that Parks had a deep belief 'that integration was a positive good for society, and she went home with a determination to do her part to end Jim Crow'.[18] Although she had not planned her action that evening she was obviously aware of the consequences that might follow and was prepared to face arrest and imprisonment in order to attract attention to the cause in which she fervently believed. The news of her arrest spread rapidly throughout the local community and the local leader of the NAACP, E.D. Nixon, paid the bail money necessary for her release from jail. A friend of Parks, Jo Ann Robinson, an English professor at Alabama State College and head of the Women's Political Council, who had campaigned for desegregation of the buses, was informed by Nixon of Parks' arrest late on Thursday night. Realizing the opportunity this presented she assembled a few helpers and composed a short manifesto, then 'working throughout the night over a mimeograph machine at Alabama State College . . . printed thousands of flyers' announcing a boycott of the buses on the following Monday.[19] Robinson and other members of the Women's Political Council distributed these leaflets throughout the black areas of Montgomery the following day. Meanwhile

Nixon was attempting to contact local ministers of the Baptist churches in Montgomery to enlist their help in supporting the boycott. He first called his own minister, Rev. Abernathy, who 'responded positively' and suggested that Nixon should contact the new minister, Rev. Martin Luther King Jr. Brinkley records that 'to Nixon's surprise, King proved cautious and did not jump on the boycott bandwagon right away, hedging even on endorsing it. "Brother Nixon," King said, "let me think about it and call you back"'.[20] Abernathy eventually persuaded King to join with them in supporting the boycott, and Nixon called a meeting for the Friday evening to discuss plans. King's account of the events of Friday, December 2, are very different to those described above, the most obvious difference being the total lack of any reference to Jo Ann Robinson and the members of the Women's Political Council. Robinson had been the first person to suggest a boycott of the buses, declaring, after Parks' arrest, 'the women of Montgomery will call for a boycott to take place on Monday, December 5'.[21] She had then spent all night composing and printing thousands of leaflets. King writes in his autobiography that his response to Nixon's phone call was to agree immediately that 'protest was necessary and that the boycott method would be an effective one', and to offer his church for the Friday evening meeting.[22] While Robinson was busy planning and publicizing the boycott, the ministers and local black leaders agreed that it was time to act and appointed a committee to prepare a statement. The statement which King refers to as 'our message' was actually a shorter version of the statement written and already distributed by Robinson, using her exact words. Rosa Parks in *My Story* describes how Robinson and some of her students had distributed leaflets to all the local schools on Friday morning 'so that students could take them home to their parents'. She also notes how the leaflet prepared by the ministers on Friday evening 'was basically a condensation of the leaflet that Jo Ann Robinson and the others . . . had written'.[23] The question arises as to why King ignored Robinson's vital role in the boycott and why he wished to give the impression that it was he and the other Baptist ministers who had called for the boycott, rather than just agreeing to support Robinson's initiative. The simple answer to this question is that the Baptist churches in the South, as Ella Baker had noted, were hierarchical and completely male dominated, and it would have been impossible for them to acknowledge that a group of women possessed sufficient strength, ability and influence to plan and organize the bus boycott. It was, of course, mainly women who used the buses to get to their places of work, and the boycott could be seen as a mass popular protest of the type envisaged by Ella Baker. However, Nixon, together with local dignitaries and pastors, considered that this protest would need to have a leader and naturally this leader would be male. They agreed to form an organization called the Montgomery Improvement Association (MIA), and on the first day of the boycott met together to elect a leader. Many of the clergy present were apprehensive about supporting the boycott, afraid that they might be accused of being Communist sympathizers and be removed from their posts. Nixon accused them of being "scared little boys", saying "if we're going to be men, now's the time to be men". Moye comments that 'the gendered language he chose was interesting, because he had failed to invite the women who were responsible for the boycott in the first place'. Jo Ann Robinson later commented that "The men took it over".[24] It was assumed that either Nixon or Abernathy would be elected as leader, but the majority were apprehensive about what they perceived as Nixon's overambitious demands for the ending of the boycott. After Nixon's outburst, King stood up in support of the other ministers saying 'Brother Nixon, I'm not a coward' and viewing him as an uncontroversial choice the meeting voted him in as leader. That evening King delivered a speech at the Holt Street Baptist Church, a speech which Moye describes as 'one of the greatest speeches in the entire history of American protest rhetoric',[25] and from that moment he began his journey towards becoming America's greatest 'hero'.

As the leader of the MIA, King played a considerable role in the organization of the boycott using his church contacts to arrange car pools and private taxis to take people to work. However, it was black women like Jo Ann Robinson who undertook the day-to-day running of the car pool, who staffed the MIA office and who organized fund-raising events. Brinkley notes that 'Jo Ann Robinson was in her usual over-drive, managing every facet of the protest, from editing the newsletter to driving one of the car pools every day . . . as MIA financial secretary Ema Dungee recalled it was women activists who "passed the ideas to men to a great extent"'.[26] King does acknowledge the role played by Robinson but in a somewhat condescending manner, says 'another loyal driver was Jo Ann Robinson. Attractive, fair-skinned, and still youthful, Jo Ann came by her goodness naturally. She did not need to learn her nonviolence from any book'.[27] Far from simply being a 'loyal driver', Jo Ann Robinson had played a pivotal part in initiating and organizing the boycott. In 1984, the historian David Garrow, while searching through documents in Montgomery, came across a letter dated May 1954, which Robinson had written to the Mayor of Montgomery threatening to organize a boycott of the buses, and Garrow realized 'that Robinson and the women of Montgomery were the true boycott organizers', although Robinson was reluctant to claim credit for what she had done.[28] Lynne Olson, in her book about women in the Civil Rights Movement, says 'looking back on the boycott, Mary Fair Burks compared the contribution made by Martin Luther King, Jr., with that of the women of Montgomery: "A trailblazer is a pioneer in a field of endeavor. A torchbearer . . . indicates one who follows the trail-blazer. Rosa Parks, Jo Ann Robinson and members of the Women's Political Council were trailblazers. Martin Luther King, Jr., was a torchbearer"'.[29]

Perhaps if the word 'hero' was to be applied to anyone during the boycott it would be to the thousands of black women and men who risked their jobs, their livelihoods, their homes, who faced threats and often violence from local white groups and from the police, who walked up to twelve miles a day often in severe winter weather, all for a cause which would enable them to be recognized as equal members of the human race.

Ella Baker had been following events in Montgomery from New York and her 'In Friendship' organization had raised money for the MIA. Baker was overwhelmed by the massive response to the boycott viewing it as the first example of the type of action she had been working towards, a spontaneous mass response made by people acting locally to solve a problem which directly affected them. After the successful completion of the boycott Baker, Rustin and Levison went to Montgomery hoping to encourage the MIA to spread the idea of mass action throughout the South, but as John A. Kirk notes in his study of King 'despite his expenditure of time and energy, King failed to maintain the momentum of the bus boycott in Montgomery, and to expand black activism across the South'.[30] Baker commented, 'I don't think that the leadership in Montgomery was prepared to capitalize . . . on what had come out of the Montgomery situation'.[31]

Baker, Rustin and Levison suggested to King that a new civil rights organization should be formed which would encourage more mass direct action campaigns, building on the success of the bus boycott, and in January 1957 King met with other black ministers to form the Southern Christian Leadership Conference (SCLC). The inclusion of 'Christian' in the title indicated that this organization would be very much church led, and this meant that decisions would be made by the ministers rather than by members of the congregations, the top-down model that Baker had warned would fail to stimulate ideas for mass action. It would also exclude women from decision making, a fact that did not concern the overtly chauvinistic black preachers who had failed to acknowledge the vital role played by women in the bus boycott. Despite this, on the recommendation of Rustin and Levison, Baker was appointed as administrator for the SCLC, even though, according to Moye, 'King, who seems to have considered the term *professional woman* an oxymoron, doubted a female could be effective in the role'.[32] Baker began to build up a network of support, travelling throughout the South, hiring speakers, arranging local meetings and seeking publicity for a proposed 'Crusade for Citizenship', the aim of which was to encourage voter registration. This did meet with some success but Baker soon came to realize how much King dominated the SCLC, and how it was failing 'to encourage a democratic mass movement'. Fairclough notes that 'not only was the SCLC synonymous with King, but also the organization promoted a personality cult that grew to excessive proportions . . . the SCLC's history consisted largely of King's comings and goings: King meeting . . . President Eisenhower, King attending Ghana's independence ceremonies . . . King receiving awards and honors. King's willingness to occupy centre stage suggested, to Baker, a reprehensible degree of egotism and self-importance'.[33] Years later she wrote 'because a person is called upon to give public statements and is acclaimed by the establishment, such a person gets to the point of believing that he *is* the movement. Such people get so involved with playing the game of being important that they exhaust themselves and their time and they don't do the work of actually organizing people'. Baker was certainly not the only associate of King to make such comments.[34]

It is perhaps important here to point out that much of this 'heroization' of King was not his fault, but was a result of the way in which his personal characteristics conformed with people's ideas of what a 'hero' should be. As Zimbardo and others have suggested, his social standing, leadership ability, communication skills and above all the publicity he received, all contributed to his acceptance as the major 'hero' of the Civil Rights Movement, whereas there were many other less charismatic, less articulate people who made a greater contribution and who sacrificed more and yet remained unrecognized. King was intelligent and well educated, most of his later education being in white-dominated, middle-class institutions. He was gifted at oratory, capable of producing strong emotional responses in those who listened to his sermons and speeches. He was deeply religious, believing that he had been called by God to 'stand up for righteousness' and justice. He says 'I tell you I've seen the lightning flash. I've heard the thunder roar . . . I heard the voice of Jesus saying still to fight on. He promised never to leave me alone'.[35] He strongly believed that the people needed a leader, that they would not be capable of acting on their own, and writing in his autobiography he describes his thoughts before his speech at the Holt Street Baptist Church, saying 'how could I make a speech that would be militant enough to keep my people aroused to positive action and yet moderate enough to to keep their fervor within controllable Christian bounds? I knew that many of the Negro people were victims of bitterness that could easily rise to flood proportions'.[36] King's reference to 'my people' and 'arousing them to action' does make him sound like a traditional heroic leader, and this is obviously how he appeared to those listening to his speech. His view that the Negro people might be unable to control themselves leading to 'un-Christian' behavior is somewhat condescending, and reflects King's belief that it was the churches and their Christian ministers that should act as the force for change. King's popularity with the people did cause some resentment amongst other black leaders. Kirk notes that after the successful ending of the boycott 'King's star rose far higher than that of any other black leader in the city. Media accounts placed King at the centre of the boycott. Even though King's account of the Montgomery bus boycott . . . was at pains to acknowledge the efforts of others, many still felt that the young preacher was unjustly emphasizing his role in events while diminishing theirs'.[37]

Baker continued to work for the SCLC, but became increasingly disillusioned with its method of working and failure to promote active campaigns. She respected King and admired 'his ability to move crowds and to communicate the goals of the civil rights movement', but she doubtless thought that 'the ability to deliver a moving speech' was not 'the most important trait a civil rights activist could develop'.[38] Baker's hope for a protest arising from the people themselves was soon to be fulfilled when on February 1, 1960, four black students from the North Carolina Agricultural and Technical College in Greensboro, North Carolina sat at the segregated lunch counter of a downtown Woolworths store and ordered coffee. The waitress refused to serve them and they were asked to leave, but they refused to give up their seats, staying until the store closed and then returning the following morning with twenty more students, the numbers rising to eighty or more over the next few days. The students were frustrated at lack of action by the NAACP and SCLC and decided that the only way to defeat segregation was by engaging in direct mass action. The sit-in protests spread to other stores and businesses with hundreds of students involved and soon spread to neighboring states with thousands of students staging sit-ins, rallies and marches. They had to face police brutality and white mob violence and as Fairclough notes, 'the students placed themselves in a vulnerable position that required considerable courage. In many places hostile whites, undeterred and even encouraged by the police, shoved, kicked and punched demonstrators . . . and thrust lighted cigarettes against their bodies'.[39] Moye reports how in Houston Texas 'angry whites ripped a black student off his stool, kidnapped him, carved KKK in his chest, and left him hanging from a tree by his knees'.[40]

Baker greeted this youth-centered mass action with enthusiasm but was concerned that it might be taken over by the leaders of the NAACP, SCLC and other organizations, rather than allowing the students to make their own decisions and plan their own actions. King did support the student movement and gave an inspiring speech at a conference at Shaw University, organized by Baker. Although not as charismatic as King, Baker had 'no difficulty relating to the young people' and 'spoke simply but powerfully'. They had, of course, all heard of King, regarding him as a celebrity, but few of them were fully aware of Baker's contribution to the civil rights movement and were consequently very impressed when they realized how closely her ideas on mass protest corresponded with their own. Few people would recognize the names of the students who initiated the sit-in protest, suffering physical and verbal abuse for their cause, yet within a few months their actions resulted in the desegregation of store lunch counters in towns and cities across the South.[41] With Baker's encouragement the students at the Shaw conference decided to form their own protest group, the Student Nonviolent Coordinating Committee (SNCC), based on non-hierarchical, democratic principles with decisions made as a result of group discussions rather than by a few leaders. Ella Baker remained as a respected adviser in an organization which encouraged women to play an active role and which was to 'forge the agenda for the civil rights movement' in the sixties. King still played a role but in the words of John Kirk 'by 1961 he was in danger of falling behind so far that he risked becoming merely a bystander in unfolding events'.[42] Putting Baker's theories into practice, SNCC members moved into communities 'to help the local people help themselves; their job was to empower local people to make their own decisions, not impose decisions on them'.[43]

One young SNCC member who had taken part in the sit-in protests and had attended the Shaw University conference was John Lewis, who in May 1961, played an important part in the Freedom Rides, one of the most significant and successful anti- segregation protests, a saga of 'heroic sacrifice and unexpected triumph'.[44] The idea for the Freedom Rides originated with members of the Congress of Racial Equality (CORE) who had undertaken a Journey of Reconciliation through the upper Southern states in 1947. In 1961, despite rulings made by the US Supreme Court outlawing segregation on public transport, local segregation laws persisted on buses and in bus stations, particularly in Deep South states such as Georgia and Alabama. Lewis had learned about the Freedom Ride from an advertisement in the SNCC newsletter, *The Student Voice*, and on May 4, the twenty-one year old would-be preacher joined the racially mixed group of thirteen Riders at the Greyhound bus station in Washington, D.C. The Riders encountered few problems as they travelled through Virginia and North Carolina but on arriving at the bus station in the town of Rock Hill in South Carolina, Lewis was confronted by a group of white supremacists as he approached the "White" waiting room and was punched to the floor and then kicked. Two other Riders tried to intervene but they were also attacked and 'shaken and bleeding . . . staggered into the terminal restaurant to join the rest of the Riders. Lewis, who had suffered bruised ribs and severe cuts around his eyes and mouth, was in need of medical attention . . . but throughout the whole ordeal he downplayed his injuries . . . displaying the quiet courage for which he would later become famous'.[45] John Lewis and the other Freedom Riders certainly showed courage in Rock Hill but they were to be tested to a far greater extent a few days later when the bus crossed the border into Alabama. Before entering Alabama they had received a brief visit from

Martin Luther King Jr. in Atlanta on his way back from attending a SCLC meeting in Montgomery. King had, of course, played no part in this protest but as Arsenault says 'the SCLC leader was at his gracious best, repeatedly praising the Freedom Riders for their courage'. Indeed some of the Riders 'began to hope that he might join them on the bus the following morning, but they soon learned that King had no intention of becoming a Freedom Rider'. King had in fact confided to one of the reporters covering the Ride that 'SCLC sources had uncovered evidence of a plot to disrupt the ride with violence', and he warned the Riders that they would not make it through Alabama.[46] The Riders refused to be deterred and were determined to continue with their demonstration of nonviolent resistance. They departed from the bus station in Atlanta the following morning, unaware that the Ku Klux Klan, having been informed of their plans by the local police department, were waiting for them in the town of Anniston, Alabama. As the bus entered the bus station a mob of about fifty Klan members 'carrying metal pipes, clubs and chains' surrounded it, and proceeded to smash the windows, slash the tyres and throw rocks through the broken windows. Fortunately the Riders had managed to seal the doors of the bus but when the police eventually arrived they made no arrests and engaged in 'friendly banter' with the Klan members. The bus managed to leave the town but on an isolated stretch of highway was surrounded by a long line of cars and trucks containing Klan members. One group attempted to turn the bus over while others smashed the few remaining windows while two highway patrolmen made no effort to intervene. Frustrated by the fact that they had been unable to force the Riders to leave the bus, two members of the mob threw a bundle of burning rags through a broken window and the bus was soon filled with thick, black smoke. Unable to breathe the Riders and other passengers were forced to leave the bus before it was engulfed in flames, and as they dragged themselves away from danger several black students were viciously attacked before the mob retreated. Undeterred by news of this violence a following group of Riders continued towards Birmingham, Alabama despite the fact that their bus had been boarded by a group of Klansmen in Atlanta. The black Riders were verbally abused and ordered to move to the back of the bus, and when they refused they were dragged from their seats and punched and kicked. Two white Riders, Jim Peck and Walter Bergman, rushed forward to defend them and were beaten by the Klansmen until 'blood spurted from their faces'. Peck was punched in the face until he lost consciousness and Bergman already unconscious was kicked in the chest. On arriving at the bus station in Birmingham further vicious attacks occurred with no intervention by the local police. Later, when Peck was being treated in hospital for deep gashes in his head he was questioned by reporters, and when asked about his plans for the future he courageously replied "the going is getting rougher, but I'll be on that bus tomorrow headed for Montgomery".[47] Unfortunately most members of the group were too badly injured to continue but SNCC members from the first bus did continue the Freedom Ride to Montgomery where the students, including John Lewis, were attacked and badly beaten by a large mob of white extremists at the bus terminal. The Attorney-General, Robert Kennedy, who up to then had made no attempt to intervene to stop the violent attacks, demanded the Alabama governor to provide tighter security and eventually agreed to send US Marshalls to Montgomery to disperse the crowds. His decision was no doubt influenced by the reaction of the millions of Americans who were becoming aware of the situation in the South. As Arsenault points out, 'the dramatic words and images of martyrdom coming out of Alabama proved irresistible beyond anything the civil rights struggle had yet produced . . . nothing it seemed had prepared Americans for the image of the burning bus outside of Aniston, or of the broken bodies in Birmingham', and the realization 'that a group of American citizens had knowingly risked their lives to assert the right to sit together on a bus'.[48]

Jim Zwerg, one of the white Freedom Riders who was seriously injured in Montgomery after being kicked in the back and repeatedly punched in the face, spoke to reporters from his hospital bed, saying 'these beatings cannot deter us from our purpose. We are not martyrs or publicity-seekers. We want only equality and justice, and we will get it . . . we are prepared to die'.[49] These Freedom Riders did not consider themselves as heroes, and were certainly not considered to be heroes by the majority of people in the states through which they passed, many of whom viewed the Riders as Communist inspired agitators. Martin Luther King Jr. and other members of the SCLC had initially been reluctant to support the Freedom Rides, but King eventually agreed to lead a mass meeting at the First Baptist Church in Montgomery, having been assured by Kennedy that US Marshalls would be there to provide protection. Some young SNCC members had misgivings about this, concerned that using King's 'prestige and celebrity to shore up the Freedom Ride was hardly in keeping with SNCC's . . . democratic ethos'.[50]

When the decision was made to continue the Freedom Ride into Mississippi, Diane Nash, a young SNCC activist, tried to persuade King to accompany them on the journey, 'insisting that he had a moral responsibility to do so'. She had been encouraged to press King on this matter by Ella Baker who was still a senior SNCC advisor. King refused, using the excuse that he was still on probation and that any additional arrest might result in a long prison sentence. Several of the students pointed out to King 'that many of them were violating their own probation terms from the sit-ins by taking part in the Freedom Ride'.[51] King 'brought the discussion to an abrupt end with the insistence that only he could decide the "time and place" of his "Golgotha", a somewhat unfortunate 'allusion to Christ's martyrdom' which led to one disappointed student referring to King as "De Lawd", 'a mocking reference to King's assumption of Christ-like status'.[52] King did give a speech in front of reporters as the Riders departed for Mississippi, saying that he would not like to see anyone die but that he was sure 'these students are willing to face death if necessary'. Arsenault notes that this emotional speech 'reinforced the public misconception that he was the supreme leader and chief architect of the Freedom Rides. In truth, he had never been a central figure in the Freedom Rider saga, and his refusal to join the Mississippi Ride had further marginalized his position among the student activists in Montgomery'.[53] Because of his charismatic personality, religious fervor and leadership and communication skills, King conformed with the idea of what a hero should be, and his acceptance as such by those listening to his speech is an example of the type of myth formation described by Roland Barthes. The image and personality of King identified him as a hero and as Barthes points out, 'it does not matter if one is later allowed to see through the myth, its action is assumed to be stronger than the rational explanations which may later belie it'. The thousands of mainly young, disadvantaged black people who actually fought to defeat segregation laws, not by delivering stirring speeches but by organizing sit-ins and Freedom Rides, were not considered to be heroes, despite the extent of the suffering they endured and the vital contribution they made to the eventual defeat of Jim Crow laws.

Six months after the start of the Freedom Rides the Interstate Commerce Commission (ICC) issued a ruling prohibiting racial segregation on interstate buses and all buses had to display a notice to this effect. However, as Ella Baker had often pointed out the value of such rulings depended on the degree of enforcement and it took a few years before many white Southerners accepted the ruling. Leaders of large organizations like the NAACP and later the SCLC believed that decisions on action should come from above and stressed the importance of federal court rulings in matters such as voting registration rights and desegregation. Baker, however, realized that change could only come when instigated by the masses and spent her working life encouraging black people to take responsibility for changing the society which oppressed them. She did not seek publicity or make great speeches but worked relentlessly with organizations such as the SNCC, helping to shape it 'into the democratic, grassroots, program-oriented civil rights organization the NAACP and SCLC could never be'.[54] King was turned into the hero of the Civil Rights movement because of his visibility and his extraordinary ability to move people with his rhetoric, at times 'merging his voice with those of Old Testament prophets in the time-honored tradition of the black clergy'. His 'I have a Dream' speech in Washington on 17 August 1963 was greeted with 'thunderous applause' and 'for one fleeting moment his vision of an integrated, beloved community appeared to be an attainable reality in America'.[55] Of course it was not a reality, but the thousands of people who fought and suffered to ensure that this reality came a little closer to being achieved are largely unremembered and unacknowledged.

One further problem highlighted by Franco, Blau and Zimbardo in their study of heroism is the existence of 'retrospective bias'. Although seen as an influential church leader and great orator who wished to see the end of segregation and inequality, King was certainly not considered to be a hero by most people in the United States during his lifetime. Many black people were opposed to his policy of non-violent protest believing that only violent action would bring about change, and a large number of poor black people in the Southern States were willing to cooperate with the Jim Crow laws fearing a backlash from extreme white groups such as the Ku Klux Klan. In the early sixties, King and fellow SCLC members were suspected of being Communist sympathizers and were under constant surveillance by the FBI, King having his phone tapped in the years leading up to his death. His opposition to the Vietnam War caused many to denounce him as being unpatriotic and a supporter of Communism. On 4 April 1968 King was killed by a rifle shot as he stood on a hotel balcony in Memphis, and the violent nature of his death played a large part in transforming him into a national hero. As Kirk observes, 'much of white America felt sympathy and remorse at King's death. President Johnson ordered flags to be flown at half mast and declared the following Sunday a national day of mourning'.[56] King's commitment to non-violence however had not brought about an end to inequality in the South and his death resulted in an outbreak of violent protest across black America. Many student members of the SNCC joined the 'Black Power' movement believing that violence was the only way to achieve their aims but this only resulted in escalation of violence across the country and an increase in antagonism between black and white communities in the South. In the end the only people who might qualify to be referred to as 'heroes', by those who find it necessary to use the word, are the thousands of ordinary black men and women who struggled and marched and suffered in order to be treated as equal citizens of the United States of America. They of course would not consider themselves to be 'heroes', just human beings.

Klapp, in his 1954 paper, observed that 'rationality should not be stressed as a factor in recognition of heroes', a process 'in which there is little reflective thought' and which makes 'some men famous and obscures others equally deserving of credit'.[57] Perhaps the 'heroization' of certain individuals serves to compensate for our own perceived feelings of powerlessness and inadequacy when in reality most of us, if called upon, would be capable of behaving in ways generally considered to be heroic.

It might appear that all aspects of behavior associated with the signifier 'hero' involve some sort of action on the part of the person being awarded that appellation, but it may also be considered that a person facing the problems of a seemingly ordinary life with courage and endurance is equally worthy of recognition, for 'daily toil on any level has its own occasions of struggle, victory, and quiet death'.[58] Nietzsche had said of his fellow human beings, 'I have no pity for them, because I wish them the only thing that can prove today whether one is worth anything or not – that one endures'.[59]

A recurring theme in the writings of W.H. Auden is the importance of 'daily toil' and endurance in a person's life rather than a search for significance in the performance of 'heroic' deeds and I conclude this study with a brief look at some of Auden's words on the subject of heroism.

In the poem 'Missing' Auden puts forward an alternative view of the hero,

> Heroes are buried who
> Did not believe in death,
> And bravery is now,
> Not in the dying breath
> But resisting the temptations
> To skyline operations.[60]

John Fuller comments that for Auden 'heroism does not lie in acts of bravery but in endurance' and that Auden concurs with the concept that 'the Truly Strong Man has no need to prove himself. Only the Truly Weak Man finds himself undertaking absurd heroics in an effort to master his real nature'.[61]

In 'Who's Who', Auden appears to trivialize the life of action and fame led by the popular hero and shows him longing for the ordinary, mundane, self-sufficient life led by the person he once loved:

A shilling life will give you all the facts:
How Father beat him, how he ran away,
What were the struggles of his youth, what acts
Made him the greatest figure of his day:
Of how he fought, fished, hunted, worked all night,
Though giddy, climbed new mountains; named a sea:
Some of the last researchers even write
Love made him weep his pints like you and me.

With all his honors on, he sighed for one
Who say astonished critics, lived at home;
Did little jobs about the house with skill
And nothing else; could whistle; would sit still
Or potter round the garden; answered some
Of his long marvellous letters but kept none.[62]

The person who is able to find significance and meaning in the ordinary and the everyday, who does not seek glory and honors in wars fought for dubious reasons, who does not seek to receive adulation for performing heroic deeds and who does not need to perform altruistic acts to gratify their ego, is indeed the 'Truly Strong Man'.

In his collection of poems grouped together under the title 'The Quest', Auden describes the mythical hero's journey during which he overcomes difficulties and aims to achieve seemingly unattainable goals. Auden's hero though is a 'false hero conducting an abortive quest: the average man who is educated to believe himself exceptional'.[63]

The pressure of their fond ambition made
Their shy and country-loving child afraid

> No sensible career was good enough,
> Only a hero could deserve such love.
>
> So here he was without maps or supplies,
> A hundred miles from any decent town;
> The desert glared into his blood-shot eyes,
> The silence roared displeasure: looking down,
> He saw the shadow of an Average Man
> Attempting the exceptional, and ran.[64]

Later in 'The Quest', the hero is bombarded with questions from the crowd who 'like the 'astonished critics' of the popular hero in the sonnet 'Who's Who' . . . cannot believe that having been the greatest figure of his day he can long for someone who does little more than potter around the garden'.[65] He refuses to take their questions about his heroic exploits seriously even though the questioners obviously feel that 'a hero owes a duty to his fame'. They lose all respect for him as a hero and,

> The only difference that could be seen
> From those who'd never risked their lives at all
> Was his delight in details and routine:
>
> For he was always glad to mow the grass,
> Pour liquids from large bottles into small,
> Or look at clouds through bits of colored glass.[66]

These last two lines do not indicate the leading of a pointless, wasted life but a life devoted to observation and aesthetics.[67] Fuller suggests that Auden's true hero accepts the limitations placed on all human actions by 'the forces of time and space', and realizes that 'one must not be anxious about ultimate success or failure but think only about what it is necessary to do at the present moment'.[68] When all human beings can be seen to possess the potential to act in ways which might be considered to be 'heroic', and the mythical signifier 'hero' has been associated with an increasing number of widely different concepts, then it is surely time for the term 'hero' to be abandoned and replaced with a range of more meaningful signifiers.

Notes

Introductory Chapter

1 Homer, *The Iliad*, Book Two, trans. Richmond Lattimore (Chicago: University of Chicago Press, 1951), p. 79.

2 George Eliot, *Middlemarch* (London: Penguin Books, 1965), p. 519.

3 John Gray, *The Silence of Animals: On Progress and Other Modern Myths* (London: Penguin Books, 2013), p. 98.

4 Roland Barthes, *Mythologies* (London: Vintage, 2009), pp. 131–2.

5 Ibid., p. 139.

6 Barthes, *Mythologies*, p. 155.

7 Joseph Campbell, *The Hero With a Thousand Faces* (London: Fontana Press, 1993), p. 3.

8 Joseph Campbell with Bill Moyers, *The Power of Myth* (New York: Doubleday, 1988), p. 132.

9 Gray, *The Silence of Animals*, p. 118.

10 Christian Roesler, 'Are archetypes transmitted more by culture than biology? Questions arising from conceptualizations of the archetype', *Journal of Analytical Psychology*, 57 (2012), 223–246.

11 Roesler, p. 231.

12 Northrop Frye, *Anatomy of Criticism* (London: Penguin Books, 1990), p. 186.

13 Frye, p. 187.

14 Claude Lévi-Strauss, *The Raw and the Cooked: Introduction to a Science of Mythology*, vol. 1 (New York: Penguin, 1986), p. 12.

15 See Edmund Leach, *Lévi-Strauss* (London: Fontana, 1970), pp. 18–20 for a critique of Lévi-Strauss' methods.

16 Hegel, *The Philosophy of History* [1822] (New York: Prometheus Books, 1991), p. 30.

17 Thomas Carlyle, *On Heroes, Hero-Worship, and the Heroic in History: Six Lectures by Thomas Carlyle* (London: Chapman and Hall, 1842), p. 123.

18 Leo Tolstoy, *War and Peace* (New York: Vintage Books, 2008), p. 1087.

19 Linda Colley, *Britons: Forging the Nation 1707–1837* (London: Pimlico, 2003), p. 178.
20 Sidney Hook, *The Hero in History* [1943] (New York: Cosimo, Inc., 2008), p. 151.
21 Hook, pp. 238–9.

ONE

1 Richmond Lattimore, Introduction to Homer, *The Iliad* (Chicago: University of Chicago Press, 1951), p. 47.
2 Homer, *The Iliad*, trans. Richmond Lattimore (University of Chicago Press, 1951), Book 24, lines 41–3. Hereafter referred to by Book and line numbers in parenthesis.
3 Malcolm M. Willcock, *A Companion to The Iliad* (Chicago: University of Chicago Press, 1976), p. 179.
4 Plato, *The Republic*, trans, H.D.P. Lee (Harmondsworth, Penguin Books Ltd., 1955), pp. 128–9.
5 Plato, *The Republic*, p. 122.
6 Ibid., p. 128.
7 Ibid., pp. 128–9.
8 Angela Hobbs, *Plato and the Hero: Courage, Manliness and the Impersonal Good* (Cambridge: Cambridge University Press, 2000), p. 204.
9 Hobbs, p. 202.
10 Plato, *The Republic*, p. 121.
11 This famous speech is reproduced in full on many internet websites. See for example: http://historymatters.gmu.edu/d/6456
12 Dan Hassler-Forest, *Capitalist Superheroes: Caped Crusaders in the Neoliberal Age* (Winchester: Zero Books, 2012), p. 5.
13 Oyvind Vagnes, "Chosen to be Witness': The Exceptionalism of 9/11." Quoted in Hassler-Forest, pp. 26–7.
14 Hassler-Forest, pp. 27–30.
15 Chris Kyle, with Jim DeFelice and Scott McEwen, *American Sniper: The Autobiography of the Most Lethal Sniper in U.S. Military History* (New York: HarperCollins, 2012), p. 4.
16 Ibid., pp. 7–10.
17 Ibid., p. 54.
18 Ibid., p. 178.
19 Ibid., p. 377.
20 Ibid., pp. 282–3.
21 Ibid., p. 86.
22 Ibid., p. 194.
23 Ibid., p. 219.

24 Ibid., p. 231.

25 Hassler-Forest, p. 15.

26 Ibid., p. 43.

27 Hobbs, pp. 11–12.

28 Kyle, p. 273.

29 Hobbs, p. 213.

30 Friedrich Nietzsche, *The Genealogy of Morals* (New York: Dover Publications, Inc., 2003), p. 25.

31 Hobbs, p. 44.

32 Robert C. Solomon, 'Friedrich Nietzsche' in *Continental Philosophy*, Robert C. Solomon and David Sherman, eds (Oxford: Blackwell Publishing Ltd.,2003), p. 106.

33 Friedrich Nietzsche, *The Gay Science* (New York: Vintage Books, 1974), p. 228.

34 See Margaret Macmillan, *The War That Ended Peace: How Europe Abandoned Peace for the First World War* (London: Profile Books Ltd., 2014), pp. xxi–xxii, for a discussion of factors leading up to the outbreak of war in 1914.

35 Nietzsche, *Thus Spoke Zarathustra* (Harmondsworth: Penguin Books Ltd., 1961), p. 74.

36 Nietzsche, *Thus Spoke Zarathustra*, p. 77.

37 Thomas Hardy, *The Complete Poems* (London: Macmillan Ltd., 1976), p. 540.

38 Ibid., p. 542.

39 David Lloyd George, Speech, Queen's Hall, London (19 September, 1914), https://archive.org/stream/greatwarspeechde00lloyvoft_djvu.txt

40 Erich Maria Remarque, *All Quiet on the Western Front* (London: Mayflower-Dell, 1963), pp. 20–21.

41 Ibid., p. 42.

42 Ibid., pp. 78–9.

43 Ibid., pp. 79–80.

44 Ibid., p. 91.

45 Ibid., p. 84.

46 Ibid., pp. 125–8.

47 Ibid., p. 147.

48 Ibid., p. 148.

49 Remarque, pp. 134–6.

50 David Lloyd George, Speech at Mansion House (21 July 1911), quoted in *The Times* (22 July 1911), p. 7.

51 Remarque, p. 190.

52 Remarque, p. 143.

53 Laleh Khalili, *Heroes and Martyrs of Palestine: The Politics of National Commemoration* (Cambridge: Cambridge University Press, 2007), p. 144.
54 Claire Norton, 'Marines versus Fedayeen: Interpretive Naming and Constructing the Other', http://bad.eserver.org/issues/2003/63//norton.html
55 Khalili, p. 145.
56 Ibid., p. 146.
57 Ibid., p. 140.
58 http://usatoday30.usatoday.com/news/nation/2010
59 Khalili, p. 153.
60 Norton, 'Marines versus Fedayeen', p. 1.
61 Norton, p. 7.
62 Ibid., p. 5.
63 Kyle, *American Sniper*, p. 119.
64 Barthes, *Mythologies*, p. 156.
65 See for example, 'America's Mighty Warriors', set up in memory of US Navy Seal, Marc A. Lee.
66 Umberto Eco, 'Why Are They Laughing In Those Cages?', in *Travels in Hyperreality* (London: Pan Books Ltd, 1987), pp. 122–3.
67 Khalili, pp. 69, 117.
68 William Astore, '"Our American Heroes": Why It's Wrong to Equate Military Service with Heroism', www.commondreams.org/views/2010/07/22/

TWO

1 Khalili, pp. 92–3.
2 Ibid., p. 101.
3 Khalili, p. 93.
4 See Nachman Ben-Yehuda, *The Masada Myth: Collective Memory and Mythmaking in Israel* (The University of Wisconsin Press, 1996) for an account of the creation and development of this myth.
5 Yael Zerubavel, 'The Death of Memory and the Memory of Death: Masada and the Holocaust as Historical Metaphors', *Representations*, 45(Winter, 1994), University of California Press, pp. 75–6.
6 Zerubavel, p. 78.
7 David Ben-Gurion, speech for the Tel Hai memorial day of 1943, later published as 'Tsav Tel Hai', *Kuntres* 381 (1944): 3.
8 Zerubavel p. 80.
9 Martin Gilbert, *The Holocaust: The Jewish Tragedy* (London: Fontana Press, 1987)

10 Gilbert, p. 157, from the testimony of J. Dawidowicz, 'Revenge – Recollections of a Partisan', *Folksstime*, Warsaw, July–August 1958, recorded in Reuben Ainsztein, *Jewish Resistance in Nazi-occupied Eastern Europe*, London 1974, p. 259.
11 Gilbert, p. 184.
12 Gilbert, p. 184.
13 Article entitled 'Heroes of Nowogrodek' in *Jutrznia*, 28 March 1942. Quoted in Gilbert, pp. 300–1.
14 Emmanuel Ringelblum, notes, 17 June 1942: Joseph Kermish, 'Emmanuel Ringelblum's Notes Hitherto Unpublished': *Yad Vashem Studies*, VII, Jerusalem 1968, pp. 178–80. Quoted in Gilbert, pp. 368–9.
15 Chaim Kaplan diary, 3 July 1942, in Abraham I. Katsch (editor), *The Warsaw Diary of Chaim A. Kaplan* (New York, 1973), pp. 71–2. Quoted in Gilbert, p. 369.
16 Franciszek Zabecki, recollection typescript, p. 45 in Gilbert, p. 395.
17 Emmanuel Ringelblum, *Notes from the Warsaw Ghetto*, ed. Jacob Sloan, October 1942, p. 329.
18 Ibid., p. 207.
19 David Wdowinski, *And We Are Not Saved*, London, 1964, pp. 67–8. Quoted in Gilbert, p. 397.
20 It is also possible that lack of enthusiasm for the commemoration of Betar arises from the fact that the leader of the revolt, Simon bar Kokhba, was considered by many of his followers to be the Messiah the Jews had been waiting for.
21 Darius Libionka and Laurence Weinbaum, 'Deconstructing Memory and History: The Jewish Military Union (ZZW) and the Warsaw Ghetto Uprising', *Jewish Political Studies Review 18:1–2* (Spring 2006), p. 4.
22 Gilbert, p. 396.
23 Libionka and Weinbaum, p. 2.
24 Emmanuel Ringelbaum, *Polish-Jewish Relations during the Second World War*, eds. Joseph Kermish and Shmuel Krakoski (Jerusalem Vashem, 1974) p. 169–70, in Libionka and Weinbaum, p. 2.
25 Libionka and Weinbaum, p. 2.
26 Yanky Fachler, www.jewishireland.org/news/the-day-a-jewish-flag-flew-over-the-warsaw-ghetto (15/04/2016)
27 Libionka and Weibaum, p. 2.
28 Lucy S. Dawidowicz, *The War against the Jews 1933–1945* (New York: Holt, Rinehart and Winston, 1975), pp. 337–8, in Libionka and Weinbaum, p. 5.

29 Yitzhak Zuckerman, *Surplus of Memory*, p. 412, in Libionka and Weinbaum, p. 5.

30 Dawidowicz, pp. 262–3.

31 Libionka and Weinbaum, p. 4.

32 Ringelblum, *Notes from the Warsaw Ghetto*, p. 326.

33 Eliezer Task, 'An Escape from Treblinka': *The Community of Semiatych*, in Gilbert, p. 597.

34 For a full account of the revolt at Birkenau see Gilbert, pp. 743–50.

35 See Primo Levi, *The Drowned and the Saved* [1986] (London: Abacus, 2013), pp. 48–61.

36 These words written in Greek, are taken from a manuscript found in 1980 in a thermos flask buried near Crematorium II, by Polish schoolchildren planting a tree. The manuscript is in the Auschwitz Museum, and a copy was sent to Martin Gilbert for inclusion in his book.

37 Zivia Lubetkin, *In the Days of Destruction and Revolt*, pp. 202–3, in Gilbert, p. 563.

38 Ibid., pp. 292–3, in Gilbert, pp. 564–5.

39 Ibid., p. 288, in Gilbert, p. 565.

40 Shmuel Zygielbojm, quote from a letter in Gutman, *The Jews of Warsaw*, p. 363, in Gilbert, p. 565.

41 Judith Tydor Baumel, 'Founding Myths and Heroic Icons: Reflections on the Funerals of Theodor Herzl and Hannah Szenes', *Women's Studies International Forum*, Vol. 25, No. 6, 2002, p. 682.

42 Judith Tydor Baumel-Schwartz, *Perfect Heroes: The World War II Parachutists and the Making of Israeli Collective Memory* (Madison: The University of Wisconsin Press, 2010).

43 Zerubavel, p. 80.

44 Baumel-Schwartz, p. 44.

45 Ibid.

46 Ibid., p. 60.

47 See Baumel-Schwartz, pp. 110–17 for an account of 'The Yad Hannah Affair'.

48 Ibid., pp.104–5.

49 Barbara Winton, *If it's Not Impossible: The Life of Sir Nicholas Winton* (Kibworth Beauchamp: Matador, 2014), p. xvi.

50 Anthony Grenville, 'Doreen Warriner, Trevor Chadwick and the "Winton children", *The Association of Jewish Refugees Journal*, April, 2011, www.ajr.org.uk/index.cfm/section.journal/issue. Apr11

51 Ibid.

52 Barbara Winton, p. 30.

53 Grenville, *AJR Journal*.

54 Monica Porter, 'A Very Reluctant Hero', *Daily Express*, 26 Jan. 2011, www.winton.nildram.co.uk/Monica/

55 Porter, p. 2.

56 Ibid., p. 3.

57 Stephen Moss, 'British Schindler' Nicholas Winton: I wasn't heroic. I was never in danger', *The Guardian*, 9 November, 2014, www.theguardian.com/world/2014/nov/09, p. 2.

58 Porter, p. 2.

59 Porter, p. 1.

60 Rabbi Michael Lerner, in publisher's review of Tim Cole, *Selling the Holocaust: From Auschwitz to Schindler; How History is Bought, Packaged and Sold* (London: Routledge, Sept. 1999).

61 Susan Cohen, 'Winter in Prague: The humanitarian mission of Doreen Warriner', *The Association of Jewish Refugees Journal*, August 2011, www.ajr.org.uk/index.cfm/section.journal/issue.Aug11, p. 1.

62 Grenville, *AJR Journal*, April 2011, p. 1.

63 Doreen Warriner, 'Winter in Prague', *The Slavonic and East European Review*, Vol. 62, No. 2 (April 1984), pp. 209–40.

64 William Chadwick, *The Rescue of the Prague Refugees 1938–39* (Matador, Dec. 2010). This book is now unavailable but the Prologue from which this quotation is taken is available on Google Books.

65 Barbara Winton, *If it's Not Impossible*, p. 219.

66 Ibid., p. xvii.

67 Tim Cole, *Selling the Holocaust: From Auschwitz to Schindler; How History is Bought, Packaged and Sold* (London: Routledge, 1999).

THREE

1 Hegel, *The Philosophy of History* [1822] (New York: Prometheus Books, 1991), p. 30.

2 Herbert Spencer, *The Study of Sociology* [1873] (London: Kegan Paul, Trench and Co., 1887), pp. 34–5.

3 Sidney Hook, *The Hero in History* [1943] (New York: Cosimo, Inc., 2008), pp. 72–3.

4 George L. Mosse, *The Crisis of German Ideology: Intellectual Origins of the Third Reich* [1964] (New York: Howard Fertig, Inc., 1998), p. 4.

5 C.G. Jung, *Essays on Contemporary Events: Reflections on Nazi Germany* [1946] (London: Ark Paperbacks, 1988), p. 3.

6 Andrew Samuels, Foreword to C.G. Jung, *Essays on Contemporary Events*, p. x.

7 Mosse, p. 67.

8 Christopher B. Krebs, *A Most Dangerous Book: Tacitus's Germania*

from the Roman Empire to the Third Reich (New York: W.W.Norton and Co., 2011).

9   Ibid., pp. 81–2.

10 Ibid., p. 88.

11 Tacitus, *On Britain and Germany*, trans. H. Mattingly (Harmondsworth: Penguin Books Ltd., 1948), p. 101.

12 Ibid., pp. 103–4. Hereafter cited as *Germania* with page numbers in parenthesis.

13 Krebs, p. 105.

14 Ibid., p. 105

15 Ibid., p. 110.

16 Tacitus, *Annals* Book 1, http://www.sacred-texts.com/cla/tac/a01050.htm. Accessed 10/3/2016, (55), p. 4, (58), p. 7, (59), p. 8.

17 Ibid., Book 2 (9), p. 6, (10), p. 1.

18 Krebs, p. 130.

19 Mosse, pp. 4–5.

20 Ibid., p. 71.

21 Ibid., p. 172.

22 Ibid., p. 74.

23 Ian Kershaw, *The 'Hitler Myth': Image and Reality in the Third Reich* (Oxford; Oxford University Press, 1987), pp. 13, 19.

24 Joseph Goebbels, Speech at the 1927 Nuremberg Rally, http://research.calvin.edu/german-propaganda-archive/rpt27cl.htm

25 Adolf Hitler, *Mein Kampf*, trans. James Murphy (CreateSpace Independent Publishing Platform, 2014), p. 246.

26 Adolf Hitler, "Appeal to the German People" (January 31, 1933), http://germanhistorydocs.ghi-dc.org/sub_document.cfm?document id=3940.

27 Mosse, p. viii.

28 Stephen Brockmann, *Nuremberg: The Imaginary Capital* (London: Camden House, 2006), p. 145.

29 Mosse, p. 207.

30 Krebs, p. 226.

31 Ibid., p. 235.

32 Hitler, *Mein Kampf*, p. 233.

33 Ibid., p. 271.

34 Quoted in Krebs, p. 218.

35 Krebs, pp. 218–19.

36 G.W.F. Hegel, "The Positivity of the Christian Religion," in *Early Theological Writings*, trans. T.M. Knox and Richard Kroner (Philadelphia: University of Pennsylvania Press, 1948), pp. 146–7, in

George S. Williamson, *The Longing for Myth in Germany* (University of Chicago Press, 2004), p. 72.

37 Williamson, p. 73.
38 Ibid., p. 84.
39 Ibid., p. 180.
40 Hitler, *Mein Kampf*, p. 18.
41 Adolf Hitler quoted in Albert Speer, *Spandau: The Secret Diaries*, trans. R. Winston (Harper Collins Distribution Services, 1976), p. 88.
42 Roger Scruton, *The Ring of Truth: The Wisdom of Wagner's "Ring of the Nibelung"* (Allen Lane:2016), p. 30.
43 Scruton, p. 32.
44 Roland Barthes 'Myth Today', in *Mythologies* (London: Vintage Books, 2009), p. 131.
45 Scruton, p. 1.
46 Joachim Köhler, *Wagner's Hitler: The Prophet and his Disciple*, trans. Ronald Taylor (Cambridge: Polity Press, 2000).
47 Joachim Köhler, 'Wagner's Acquittal', *The Wagner Journal*, 8, 2, 43–51.
48 Ibid., pp. 46–7.
49 Ibid., p. 44.
50 Joseph Horowitz, 'The Specter of Hitler in the Music of Wagner, *The New York Times*, November 8, 1998.
51 For a fuller comparison of this poster with the illustrations made by the Bayreuth artist, Franz Stassen of Parsifal, see William Kinderman, 'Two visions of the end in Wagner's *Parsifal*', http://blog.oup.com/2013/03/richard-wagner-parsifal-stassen-lorenz/
52 See Introductory Chapter, p. 3.
53 Kinderman, p. 1.
54 Ibid., p. 3.
55 William Kinderman, *Wagner's Parsifal* (Oxford University Press, USA, 2013), p. 11.
56 Ibid., p. 20.
57 Scruton, p. 20.
58 Wagner, *Siegfried*, Act 1, Scene 3.
59 Scruton, p. 278.
60 Albrecht Classen, 'The Downfall of a Hero: Siegfried's Self-Destruction and the End of Heroism in the "Nibelungenlied", *German Studies Review*, Vol. 26, No. 2 (May, 2003), p. 302.
61 Scruton, p. 278.
62 Classen, p. 304.
63 Scruton, p. 278.

64 Alex Ross, 'Secret Passage – Decoding ten bars in Wagner's "Ring", *The New Yorker*, April 25, 2011.

65 Kershaw, p. 13.

66 Kershaw, p. 20.

67 Williamson, p. 293.

68 C.G. Jung, 'The Fight with the Shadow', *Essays on Contemporary Events*. p. 6.

69 C.G. Jung, *Memories, Dreams, Reflections*, ed., Aniela Jaffé, trans., Richard and Clara Winston (London: Fontana Press, 1993), pp. 204–5.

70 http://www.rwagner.net/libretti/siegfried/e-sieg-a3s3

71 Richard Noll, *The Jung Cult: The Origins of a Charismatic Movement* (London: Fontana Press, 1996), pp. 89–90.

72 Nietzsche, *Thus Spoke Zarathustra*, trans. R.J. Hollingdale (Harmondsworth: Penguin Books Ltd., 1961), p. 41.

73 Robert C. Solomon, 'Friedrich Nietzsche', *Continental Philosophy* (Oxford: Blackwell Publishing Ltd., 2003), pp. 105–6.

74 Robert Wicks, *Nietzsche* (Oxford: Oneworld Publications, 2002), p. 129.

75 Nietzsche, *Nietzsche Contra Wagner* (Digireads.com Publishing, 2013), p. 29.

76 Scruton, pp. 296–7.

77 Kershaw, p. 14.

78 J.P. Stern, 'Hitler. The Fuhrer and the People' (London: 1975), p. 111, quoted in Kershaw, p. 4.

79 Kershaw, p. 4.

FOUR

1 Selwyn W. Becker and Alice H. Eagly, 'The Heroism of Women and Men', *American Psychologist* 59 (3): 163–78, May 2004, p. 164.

2 Herbert Spencer, *The Study of Sociology* [1873] (London: Kegan Paul, Trench and Co., 1887), p. 31.

3 Oleg Smirnov, Holly Arrow, Douglas Kennett and John Orbell, 'Ancestral War and the Evolutionary Origins of "Heroism"', *The Journal of Politics*, Vol. 69, No. 4, November 2007, pp. 927–940.

4 Ibid., p. 928.

5 Quoted in David G. Rand and Ziv G. Epstein, 'Risking Your Life without a Second Thought: Intuitive Decision-Making and Extreme Altruism', http://journals.plos.org/plosone/article?id =10.1371/journal.pone.0109687, p. 2.

6 Rand and Epstein, p. 2.

7 Ibid., p. 5

8   Ibid.

9   Andrea Kuszewski, 'Walking the Line Between Good and Evil: The Common Thread of Heroes and Villains', *Scientific American*, March 31, 2011.

10 Kuszewski, p. 2.

11 See Marsh, Finger, Mitchell, Reid, Sims et al. 'Reduced amygdale response to fearful expressions in children and adolescents with callous—unemotional traits and behaviour disorders', *Am J Psychiatry*, 2008; 165, 712–20. Also see Antonio Damasio, *Descartes' Error* (New York: Putnam,1994), p. 209 for his description of working with a patient with damage to the pre-frontal cortex.

12 See Paul J. Zak, Angela A. Stanton, Sheila Ahmadi, 'Oxytocin Increases Generosity in Humans', *Plos One*, November 7, 2007, https://doi.org/10.1371/journal.pone.0001128.

13 See Linda Owen, *Distorting the Past: Gender and the Division of Labor in the European Upper Paleolithic* (Tübingen: Kerns Verlag, 2005), for an account of the part played by women in small game hunting and fishing.

14 Becker and Eagly, p. 7

15 Becker and Eagly, p. 13.

16 See Batrinos M.L., 'Testosterone and Aggressive Behavior in Man', *Int. J. Endocrinol Metab*. 2012, 10(3), 563–8.

17 For a full account of their experimental methods and results see Becker and Eagly, 2004, pp. 8–11.

18 Eva Fogelman, *Conscience and Courage: Rescuers of Jews during the Holocaust* (London: Cassell, 1995).

19 Fogelman, pp. 79–80.

20 Fogelman, p. 196.

21 Fogelman, p. 302.

22 For an account of this experiment see http://www.prisonexp.org

23 Zeno Franco, Philip Zimbardo, 'The Banality of Heroism', September 1, 2006, p. 2, in *Greater Good: the Science of a Meaningful Life*: http://greatergood.berkley.edu/article/item/ the_banality_of_heroism.

24 Ibid., p. 6.

25 Ibid., p. 3.

26 See Zeno E Franco, Kathy Blau and Philip G Zimbardo, 'Heroism: A Conceptual Analysis and Differentiation Between Heroic Action and Altruism', *Review of General Psychology*, 2011, Vol. 15, No. 2, p. 111.

27 Franco, Zimbardo, 2006, p. 4.

28 Ibid., p. 5.

29 Ibid., p. 6.
30 Franco, Zimbardo, 2006, p. 6.
31 Franco, Blau, Zimbardo, 2011, p. 99.
32 For a detailed description of this study see Franco, Blau and Zimbardo, 2011, pp. 104–109.
33 For example, films such as 'Erin Brockovich', (2000) which portrayed a citizen's confrontation with an energy company whose processes were polluting local water supplies with carcinogenic chemicals.
34 Pallone, N.J. and Henessy, J.J, 'Counterfeit courage: Toward a process psychology paradigm for the "Heroic rescue fantasy"', *Current Psychology*, June 1998, Volume 17, Issue 2, pp. 197–209.
35 Franco, Blau, Zimbardo, 2011, p. 111.
36 Franco, Blau, Zimbardo, p. 111.
37 Ibid., p. 99.
38 Ibid., p. 111.
39 Clint Wilkins, 'Heroic Imagination Project', *American Psychological Association, Psychology Teacher Network*, November 2012, http://www.apa.org/ed/precollege/ptn/2012/11/heroic-imagination.aspx
40 See https://www.gov.uk/government/publications/national-curriculum-in-england-citizenship-programes-ofstudy.
41 Philip Zimbardo, 'Understanding Heroism', part of a presentation entitled 'Heroic Imagination Project', 2011.
42 Elizabeth Svoboda, *What Makes a Hero?:The Surprising Science of Selflessness* (New York: Penguin Group, 2014), p. 139.
43 Svoboda, p. 139.
44 Ibid.
45 Ibid., p. 119.
46 Ibid., p. 106.
47 Joseph Campbell, with Bill Moyers, *The Power of Myth*, pp. 144–5.
48 'The Rise and Future of Heroism Science', 11–12 July 2016, Murdoch University, Australia, https://heroismscience.wordpress.com/conferences/1094-2/
49 Anna Freud, *The Ego and the Mechanisms of Defense* (New York: International Universities Press, 1946)
50 Beth J. Seelig and Lisa S. Rosof, 'Normal and Pathological Altruism', *Journal of the American Psychoanalytic Association*, 2001, 49:933, http://apa.sagepub.com/content/49/3/933, p. 933.
51 See Preston, S.D. 'The origins of altruism in offspring care', *Psychological Bulletin*, 139 (6), 2013, March 4, 1305–1341.
52 Seelig and Rosof, p. 947.

53 Ibid., pp. 934, 948.
54 Ibid., pp. 934–5.
55 Ibid., p. 937.
56 Seelig and Rosof, p. 948.
57 Sigmund Freud, 'The Basic Writings of Sigmund Freud' (New York: The Modern Library, 1938), p. 939, quoted in Walter Kaufmann, *Nietzsche: Philosopher, Psychologist, Antichrist* [1950] (Princeton: Princeton University Press, 1974), p. 182.
58 Friedrich Nietzsche, *The Genealogy of Morals* (New York: Dover Publications, Inc., 2003), p. 17.
59 Nietzsche, *The Dawn of Day*, trans. J.M. Kennedy (New York: Dover Publications, Inc., 2007), p. 138.
60 Kaufmann, p. 368.
61 Nietzsche, *The Dawn*, p. 141.
62 Ibid.
63 Ibid., p. 128.
64 Ibid.
65 Ibid., p. 142.
66 Nietzsche, *The Will to Power*, ed. Walter Kaufmann (New York: Vintage Books, 1968), p. 412.
67 Nietzsche, *The Will to Power*, p. 162.

FIVE

1 For an account of this incident see Ministry of Defense Citation, 21 March 2011, https://www.gov.uk/government/news/the-outstanding-examples-of-a-generation-the-op-honours-recipients
2 Richard Van Emden, *The Soldier's War:The Great War through Veteran's Eyes* (London: Bloomsbury Publishing plc, 2008), pp. 190–5.
3 Richard Van Emden, pp. 313–14.
4 Angela Hobbs, *Plato and the Hero: Courage, Manliness and the Impersonal Good* (Cambridge: Cambridge University Press, 2000), p. 213.
5 Winston Groom, *Forest Gump* (London: Black Swan Books, 1994).
6 Franco, Blau, Zimbardo, 2011, p. 110.
7 O.E. Klapp, 'Heroes, villains and fools, as agents of social control', *American Sociological Review*, 19.
8 J. Todd Moye, *Ella Baker: Community Organizer of the Civil Rights Movement* (Maryland: Rowman and Littlefield, 2013), p. 2.
9 Charles Payne, 'I've Got the Light of Freedom: The Organizing Tradition and the Mississippi Freedom Struggle' (Berkeley: University of California Press, 1995), Quoted in Moye, p. 3.

10   Moye, p. 20.

11   Moye, p. 41

12   Patricia Sullivan, *Lift Every Voice: The NAACP and the Making of the Civil Rights Movement* (New York: New Press, 2009), quoted in Moye, p. 45.

13   Clayborne Carson, ed., *The Autobiography of Martin Luther King, Jr.* (London: Abacus, 2000), p. 10.

14   Charles Payne, 'Ella Baker and Models of Social Change', *Signs: Journal of Women in Culture and Society*, 1989, vol. 14, no. 4, p. 888.

15   Douglas Brinkley, *Rosa Parks: A Life* (London: Penguin Books, 2005), p. 68.

16   Moye, p. 65.

17   King, *Autobiography*, pp. 50–51.

18   Moye, p. 82.

19   Fairclough, p. 229.

20   Brinkley, pp. 124–5.

21   Ibid., p. 122.

22   King, *Autobiography*, p. 51.

23   Rosa Parks with Jim Haskins, *My Story* (New York: Puffin Books, 1999), pp. 126, 129–30.

24   Moye, pp. 87–8.

25   Ibid., p. 88.

26   Brinkley, p. 147.

27   King, *Autobiography*, p. 66.

28   Lynne Olson, *Freedom's Daughters: The Unsung Heroines of the Civil Rights Movement from 1830 to 1970* (New York: Touchstone, 2001), p. 131.

29   Ibid.

30   John A. Kirk, *Martin Luther King Jr* (Harlow: Pearson Education Limited, 2005), p. 41.

31   Quoted in Olson, p. 133.

32   Moye, p. 94.

33   Fairclough, p. 238.

34   Ella Baker quoted in Olson, p. 144.

35   King, *Autobiography*, p. 78.

36   Ibid., p. 59.

37   Kirk, p. 39.

38   Moye, p. 105.

39   Fairclough, pp. 242–3.

40   Moye, p. 111.

41   The names of the four students who started the Greensboro sit-in

are Ezell Blair Jr., Franklin McCain, Joseph McNeil and David Richmond.

42 Kirk, p. 37.
43 Moye, p. 126.
44 Raymond Arsenault, *Freedom Riders: 1961 and the Struggle for Racial Justice* (New York: Oxford University Press, 2006), p. 4.
45 Ibid., pp. 80–81.
46 Ibid., p. 88.
47 Ibid., pp. 111–12.
48 Ibid., p. 115.
49 Ibid., p. 160.
50 Ibid., p. 161.
51 Kirk, p. 60.
52 Arsenault, p. 178.
53 Ibid., p. 179.
54 Moye, p. 134.
55 Robert Cook, *Sweet Land of Liberty?: The African-American Struggle for Civil Rights in the Twentieth Century* (Harlow, Essex: Pearson Education Limited, 1998), pp. 136–7.
56 Kirk, p. 182.
57 O.E. Klapp, 'Heroes, villains and fools, as agents of social control', *American Sociological Review,* 19, 1954, p. 59, quoted in Franco, Blau, Zimbardo, 2011, p. 110.
58 Sidney Hook, *The Hero in History*, p. 239.
59 Friedrich Nietzsche, *The Will to Power*, ed. Walter Kaufmann (New York: Vintage Books, 1968).
60 W.H. Auden, *Collected Shorter Poems, 1927–1957* (London: Faber and Faber Limited, 1966), p. 21.
61 John Fuller, *W.H. Auden: A Commentary* (London: Faber and Faber Limited, 1998), pp. 71–2.
62 W.H. Auden, *Collected Shorter Poems*, p. 78.
63 Fuller, p. 340.
64 W.H. Auden, *Collected Shorter Poems*, p. 183.
65 Fuller, p. 342.
66 W.H. Auden, *Collected Shorter Poems, p. 186.*
67 See Fuller, p. 342 for a discussion of the origins of these lines.
68 W.H. Auden, *Forwards and Afterwards*, p. 204, quoted in Fuller, p. 134.

Bibliography

Arsenault, Raymond, *Freedom Riders: 1961 and the Struggle for Racial Justice* (New York: Oxford University Press, Inc., 2006).

Auden, W. H., *Collected Shorter Poems, 1927–1957* (London: Faber and Faber Limited, 1969).

Ashby, Ruth, *Rosa Parks: Freedom Rider* (New York: Sterling Publishing Co., Inc., 2008).

Barthes, Roland, *Mythologies* (London: Vintage Books, 2009).

Baumel-Schwartz, Judith Tydor, *Perfect Heroes: The World War II Parachutists and the Making of Israeli Collective Memory* (Madison: The University of Wisconsin Press, 2010).

——, 'Founding Myths and Heroic Icons: Reflections on the Funerals of Theodor Herzl and Hannah Szenes', *Women's Studies International Forum*, Vol. 25, No. 6, 2002.

Becker, Selwyn W. and Eagly, Alice H., 'The Heroism of Women and Men', *American Psychologist* 59 (3): 163–78, May 2004.

Ben-Yehuda, Nachman, *The Masada Myth: Collective Memory and Mythmaking in Israel* (The University of Wisconsin Press, 1996).

Brinkley, Douglas, *Rosa Parks: A Life* (New York: Penguin Books, 2005).

Campbell, Joseph, *The Hero with a Thousand Faces* (London: Fontana Press, 1993).

—— with Bill Moyers, *The Power of Myth* (New York: Doubleday, 1988).

Carlyle, Thomas, *On Heroes, Hero-Worship, and the Heroic in History: Six Lectures by Thomas Carlyle* (London: Chapman and Hall, 1842).

Carson, Clayborne, ed., *The Autobiography of Martin Luther King, Jr.* (London: Abacus, 2000).

Classen, Albrecht, 'The Downfall of a Hero: Siegfried's Self-Destruction and the End of Heroism in the "Nibelungenlied"', *German Studies Review*, Vol. 26, No. 2 (May, 2003).

Cohen, Susan, 'Winter in Prague: The humanitarian mission of Doreen Warriner', http://www.ajr.org.uk/index.cfm/section.journal/issue.Aug11/article=8771

Cole, Tim, *Selling the Holocaust: From Auschwitz to Schindler; How History is Bought, Packaged and Sold* (London: Routledge, 1999).

Colley, Linda, *Britons: Forging the Nation 1707–1837* (London: Pimlico, 2003).

Cook, Robert, *Sweet Land of Liberty?: The African-American Struggle for Civil Rights in the Twentieth Century* (Harlow: Pearson Education Limited, 1998).

Cybulska, Eva, 'Nietzsche's Übermensch: A Hero of Our Time?', 2012, https://philosophynow.org/issues/93/Nietzsches_Ubermensch_A_Hero_of_Our_Time

Eco, Umberto, *Travels in Hyperreality* (London: Pan Books Ltd., 1987).

Emden, Richard van, *The Soldier's War: The Great War Through Veterans' Eyes* (London: Bloomsbury Publishing, 2008).

Fairclough, Adam, *Better Day Coming: Blacks and Equality, 1890–2000* (London: Penguin Books, 2002).

Fogelman, Eva, *Conscience and Courage: Rescuers of Jews during the Holocaust* (London: Cassell, 1995).

Franco, Zeno and Zimbardo, Philip, 'The Banality of Heroism', September 1, 2006, in *Greater Good: the Science of a Meaningful Life*: http://greatergood.berkeley.edu/article/item/the_banality_of_heroism

Franco, Zeno; Blau, Kathy and Zimbardo, Philip, 'Heroism: A Conceptual Analysis and Differentiation Between Heroic Action and Heroism', *Review of General Psychology*, 2011, Vol. 15, No. 2.

Freud, Anna, *The Ego and the Mechanisms of Defence* (New York: International Universities Press, 1946).

Frye, Northrop, *Anatomy of Criticism* (London: Penguin Books, 1990).

Fuller, John, *W.H. Auden: A Commentary* (London: Faber and Faber Limited, 1998).

Gilbert, Martin, *The Holocaust: The Jewish Tragedy* (London: Fontana Press, 1987).

Gray, John, *The Silence of Animals: On Progress and Other Modern Myths* (London: Penguin Books, 2014).

Grenville, Anthony, 'Doreen Warriner, Trevor Chadwick and the "Winton children", http://www.ajr.org.uk/index.cfm/section.journal/issue.Apr11/article=7782

Groom, Winston, *Forest Gump* (London: Black Swan, 1994).

Hassler-Forest, Dan, *Capitalist Superheroes: Caped Crusaders in the Neoliberal Age* (Alresford: Zero Books, 2012).

Hegel, *The Philosophy of History* [1822] (New York: Prometheus Books, 1991).

Hitler, Adolf, *Mein Kampf*, trans. James Murphy (Create Space Independent Publishing Platform, 2014).

Hobbs, Angela, *Plato and the Hero: Courage, Manliness and the Impersonal Good* (Cambridge: Cambridge University Press, 2000).

Homer, *The Iliad*, translated with an introduction by Richmond Lattimore (Chicago: The University of Chicago Press, 1951).

Hook, Sidney, *The Hero in History* (New York: Cosimo, Inc., 2008).

Jung, C.G., *Essays on Contemporary Events: Reflections on Nazi Germany* [1946] (London: Ark Paperbacks, 1988).

——, *Memories, Dreams, Reflections*, ed., Aniela Jaffé, trans., Richard and Clara Winston (London: Fontana Press, 1993).

Kaufmann, Walter, *Nietzsche: Philosopher, Psychologist, Antichrist* [1950] (Princeton: Princeton University Press, 2013).

Kershaw, Ian, *The 'Hitler Myth': Image and Reality in the Third Reich* (Oxford: Oxford University Press, 1989).

Khalili, Laleh, *Heroes and Martyrs of Palestine: The Politics of National Commemoration* (Cambridge: Cambridge University Press, 2007).

Kinderman, William, *Wagner's Parsifal* (Oxford University Press, USA, 2013).

Kirk, John A., *Martin Luther King, Jr.* (Harlow: Pearson Education Limited, 2005).

Klapp, O. E., 'Heroes, villains and fools, as agents of social control', *American Sociological Review*, 19, 1954.

Köhler, Joachim, *Wagner's Hitler: The Prophet and his Disciple* (Cambridge: Polity Press, 2001).

——, 'Wagner's Acquittal', *The Wagner Journal*, 8,2, 43–51.

Krebs, Christopher B., *A Most Dangerous Book: Tacitus's Germania from the Roman Empire to the Third Reich* (New York: W.W. Norton and Company, 2011).

Kuszewski, Andrea, 'Walking the Line Between Good and Evil: The Common Thread of Heroes and Villains', *Scientific American*, March 31, 2011.

Kyle, Chris, with Jim DeFelice and Scott McEwen, *American Sniper: The Autobiography of the Most Lethal Sniper in U.S. Military History* (New York: HarperCollins, 2013).

Leach Edmund, *Lévi-Strauss* (London: Fontana, 1970).

Levi Primo, *The Drowned and the Saved* (London: Abacus, 2013).

Lévi-Strauss, Claude, *The Raw and the Cooked: Introduction to a Science of Mythology*, vol. 1 (New York: Penguin, 1986), p. 12.

Libionka, Darius and Weinbaum Laurence, 'Deconstructing Memory and History: The Jewish Military Union (ZZW) and the Warsaw Ghetto Uprising', *Jewish Political Studies Review* 18: 1–2 (Spring 2006).

Macmillan, Margaret, *The War That Ended Peace: How Europe Abandoned Peace for the First World War* (London: Profile Books Ltd., 2014).

Magee, Bryan, *Aspects of Wagner* (Oxford: Oxford University Press, 1988).

Mosse, George L., *The Crisis of German Ideology: Intellectual Origins of the Third Reich* (New York: Howard Fertig, Inc., 1998).

Moye, J. Todd, *Ella Baker: Community Organizer of the Civil Rights Movement* (Lanham, Maryland: Rowman and Littlefield, 2015).

Nietzsche, Friedrich, *The Will to Power*, ed. Walter Kaufmann (New York: Vintage Books, 1968).

——, *The Dawn of Day* (New York: Dover Publications, 2007).

——, *The Gay Science* (New York: Vintage Books, 1974).

——, *The Genealogy of Morals* (New York: Dover Publications, 2003).

——, *Thus Spoke Zarathustra* (Harmondsworth: Penguin Books Ltd., 1961).

——, *Nietzsche Contra Wagner* (Digireads.com Publishing, 2013).

Noll, Richard, *The Jung Cult: Origins of a Charismatic Movement* (London: Fontana Press, 1996).

Norton, Claire, 'Marines versus Fedayeen: Interpretive Naming and Constructing the Other' (http://bad.eserver.org/issues/2003/63/norton.html)

Olson, Lynne, *Freedom's Daughters: The Unsung Heroines of the Civil Rights Movement from 1830 to 1970* (New York: Touchstone, 2002).

Pallone, N.J. and Henessy, J.J, 'Counterfeit Courage: Toward a process psychology paradigm for the "Heroic rescue fantasy"', *Current Psychology*, June 1998, Vol. 17, Issue 2.

Payne, Charles, 'Ella Baker and Models of Social Change', *Signs: Journal of Women in Culture and Society*, 1989, Vol. 15, No. 2, 99–113.

Plato, *The Republic* (Harmondsworth: Penguin Books Ltd., 1963).

Preston, S.D., 'The origins of altruism in offspring care', *Psychological Bulletin*, 139 (6), 2013, March 4, 1305–1341.

Quartz, Steven R., Sejnowski, Terrence J. *Liars, Lovers and Heroes: What the New Brain Science Reveals About How We Become Who We Are* (New York: HarperCollins, 2003).

Rand, David G. and Epstein, Ziv G., 'Risking Your Life Without a Second Thought: Intuitive Decision-Making and Extreme Altruism', *http://journals.plos.org/plosone/article?id=10.1371/journal.pone.0109687*, Oct. 15, 2014.

Ransby, Barbara, *Ella Baker and the Black Freedom Movement: A Radical Democratic Vision* (Chapel Hill: University of North Carolina Press, 2003).

Remarque, Erich Maria, *All Quiet on the Western Front* (London: Mayflower Books Ltd., 1963).

Ringelblum, Emmanuel, ed. Jacob Sloan, *Notes from the Warsaw Ghetto* (New York: McGraw-Hill Book Company, Inc., 1958).

Roesler, Christian, 'Are archetypes transmitted more by culture than biology? Questions arising from conceptualizations of the archetype'. *Journal of Analytical Psychology*, 57 (2012), 223–246.

Scruton, Roger, *The Ring of Truth: The Wisdom of Wagner's Ring of the Nibelung* (Penguin Random House UK, 2016).

Seelig, Beth J. and Rosof, Lisa S., 'Normal and Pathological Altruism', *Journal of the American Psychoanalytic Association*, 2001, 49 (3), 933–59.

Smirnov, Oleg; Arrow, Holly; Kennett Douglas and Orbell John, 'Ancestral War and the Evolutionary Origins of "Heroism"', *The Journal of Politics*, Vol. 69, No. 4, November 2007, 927–940.

Solomon, Robert C., 'Friedrich Nietzsche' in *Continental Philosophy*, Robert C. Solomon and David Sherman, eds. (Oxford: Blackwell Publishing Ltd., 2003).

Spencer, Herbert, *The Study of Sociology* [1873] (London: Kegan Paul, Trench and Co., 1887).

Svoboda, Elizabeth, *What Makes A Hero: The Surprising Science of Selflessness* (New York: Penguin Group (USA), 2014).

Tacitus, *Annals*, Books 1,2, http://www.sacred-texts.com/cla/tac/a01050.htm

——, *On Britain and Germany*, trans, H. Mattingly (Harmondsworth: Penguin Books Ltd., 1954).

Warriner, Doreen, 'Winter in Prague', *The Slavonic and East European Review*, Vol. 62, No. 2 (April 1984).

Wicks, Robert, *Nietzsche* (Oxford: Oneworld Publications, 2002).

Wilkins, Clint, 'Heroic Imagination Project', *American Psychological Association, Psychology Teacher Network*, November 2012, http://www.apa.org/ed/precollege/ptn/2012/11/heroic-imagination.aspx

Willcock, Malcolm M., *A Companion to the Iliad: Based on the Translation by Richmond Lattimore* (London: The University of Chicago Press, 1976).

Williamson, George S., *The Longing for Myth in Germany: Religion and Aesthetic Culture from Romanticism to Nietzsche* (Chicago: The University of Chicago Press, 2004).

Winton, Barbara, *If it's Not Impossible . . . : The Life of Sir Nicholas Winton* (Kibworth Beauchamp: Matador, 2014).

Zerubavel, Yael, 'The Death of Memory and the Memory of Death: Masada and the Holocaust as Historical Metaphors', *Representations*, 45 (Winter, 1994, pp. 72–100, University of California Press.

Index